NOTHIN'S ON THE SQUARE

NOTHIN'S ON THE SQUARE

82 Days on the Mayoral Campaign Trail,
Making History in Chicago 2015

MIKE HOULIHAN

Abbeyfeale

FOREWORD

*M*EETING M*IKE* H*OULIHAN* *is an experience not soon, if ever, forgotten.*

At the time, I was chronicling the hijinks of Mayor Jane Byrne, Chicago's first black mayors, Harold Washington and Eugene Sawyer and then "back to the future" Mayor Richard M. Daley.

Houlihan meanwhile, was tiring of the Broadway scene and eyeing a return to his south side roots. Mixing in the stew that is Chicago politics is a blood sport, and errors in judgment or misplaced loyalties can be fatal. Houlihan was right at home again.

"So this is Mike Houlihan," I noted when introduced by Peter Nolan, a popular TV reporter both at the CBS station and NBC's Channel 5 in Chicago. Nolan and Houlihan were teaming up to produce the political comedy "The 51st Ward".

It wasn't long before I made the decision to pull the plug. Here I was sitting across, harassing the son of Richard J. Daley, who I covered as a City Press "kid" 35 years earlier. Much of the fun and characters were gone,

Houlihan, not one to pass up an opportunity, especially involving cash, suggested I set up shop and share space with Houlihan and Nolan.

"Houli" and Nolan were a perfect match. Houlihan concocting schemes and pitches to float the coconuts and Nolan putting on the brakes before spiraling off the cliff.

The real office soon became a snug bar tucked away from gawkers making their way to the Bismarck hotel's dining room and gathering place for the city's political notables.

Here were only invited guests. Political wannabes, greats and near greats stopping by to kibitz, seek advice or scribble a note hopefully to be planted by "Houli" with press contacts.

There was no shortage of entertainment in the "Hidey Hole", a tag given our hideout to cover our movements. Houli would lay it on with a trowel in recounting his theatrical escapades and real or imagined dalliances with leading ladies. Fact or fiction he delivered every vivid episode with dramatic flair.

There was always the suspicion that Mike was stashing away the lurid tales recounted night after night, and that they would appear someday, somewhere in a Houlihan production.

In "Nothin's On The Square", Houlihan taps into politics Chicago style.

Lurking in the shadows of political campaigns is a darker side, hidden from curious observers. Here, Mike Houlihan strips away the public love-in and exposes the ugly side of campaign gamesmanship.

Gone are the days of iron rule by the Irish. Focus is on the grim fight for Chicago's City Hall in 2015, matching well-heeled liberals behind incumbent Rahm Emanuel, and an underfunded Hispanic from the political left, Jesus "Chuy" Garcia. Houlihan tells the story of a scheme to cash in on a hopeless campaign, that turns into a deep personal affection for the candidate,

—Jim Strong,
former Chicago Tribune Writer

INTRODUCTION

PLEASE FORGIVE ME for what you are about to read. It's been said that it's easier to ask forgiveness than to get permission. We shall see. I didn't start this to offend anybody, but sometimes in the telling of a tale we get carried away in the moment. Writing a book was never my intention when I hired on for this campaign, just wanted to pick up a few extra bucks. I don't expect to make more than a few on this book, but I do want to share this story with you. You don't have to like it.

Lots of folks to thank, starting with everyone I met on the campaign, both good and bad. If you were good, you inspired me. If you were bad, you made this a more interesting book.

Special thanks as well to attorney Steve Baron, who advised freely and consulted on the book with his keen intellect and judicious wit.

Also Bill Crawford, Jimmy Strong, Pete Nolan, Mike "Pickle" Joyce, Skinny Sheahan, the lovely Mary Carney, Bill and Paddy Houlihan, Mary McCloskey, Pat Fitzmaurice, Brian Coleman, Catherine O'Connell, Bob Flood, Danny Boyle, Chris Hart, Rick Kogan, Billy Wooten, Sorcha Hand, Pat Hickey, Ryan Norris, John P. Smith, Paul Peldyak, Frank Moran, Dennis Foley, Michael "Cookie" Cooke, Warner Todd Houston, Todd Musburger, Denny Kearns, William J. Kelly, John P. Smith, Roger Wolski, and anybody else who read proofs, gave feedback, or encouraged me. Lots of love to those who encouraged me. God bless you all.

I've spent almost seventy years in and around Chicago. She's my muse, my mother, my bitch. I love her. Here's my story.

It's not that the Irish are cynical. It's rather that they have a wonderful lack of respect for everything and everybody.

—Brendan Behan

PROLOGUE

I THINK I WAS in fifth or sixth grade, like 1959, when I met Mayor Richard J. Daley. I was standing by the side door of Christ the King Catholic Church on 93rd Street between Hamilton and Hoyne on the South Side of Chicago. I was with my crew of guys, loitering outside before nine o'clock Sunday mass started, spitting hockers over the bushes, hands in pockets, being wise guys, corner boys. A black car pulled up on 93rd Street and three men got out wearing suits and hats.

We gazed at them as if they were just a couple more parents heading to mass and then we were stunned by the presence of the Mayor of Chicago. To our young eyes he might as well have been The Lord God Almighty himself in our midst.

We were frozen with fear and looked at each other with our eyes bugging out. The Mare doffed his hat as he skipped up the three steps to the doors and one of his guys held the door for him. I blurted out, "Hey Mare, how's it goin'?"

"Hi ya fellas."

Huge grins broke out on our faces as we all answered Hizzoner.

"Hi Mayor!"

"Hiya Mayor Daley!"

"Thanks for coming to our parish!"

"We're White Sox fans!"

He gave a little wave as he walked through the door and all of us started going nuts, incredulous at what had just happened on the steps of CK, our parish.

His name was revered in all our homes. Our parents loved him. And so did we. He was an Irish Catholic from the South Side of Chicago. Richard J. Daley was one of us.

I was living in New York City when he died, but my world still stopped when I heard the news.

I missed the whole Mike Bilandic tenure and the Jane Byrne circus while living on the East Coast, but heard enough about her from my brother, Danny, who was sort of in her cabinet.

I had moved back to Chicago during the reign of Mayor Harold Washington, a colorful and folksy mayor who I enjoyed watching, until he died on Thanksgiving weekend of 1987. Eugene Sawyer served a couple of unremarkable years as Mayor but he never looked the part.

Then Daley's son Richard M. Daley was elected in 1989 and served even longer than his dad, when he retired in 2011.

Chicago always felt right for me with a Daley on the Fifth Floor. Rich Daley certainly wasn't anything like his old man, but he was still an Irish Catholic from the South Side.

Young Daley was a modern big city mayor, for better or worse. Shakman and a shitload of other crybabies had kinked up the old school pols that used to run this city, and many of them went to jail. But word was that Daley had cut a deal and the heir apparent was a short, cocky Clintonion, who would become Chicago's First Jewish Mayor, Rahm Emanuel

He was not one of us.

Friday January 16, 2015

Chicagoland

Sneed devotes column to her being mentioned on TV Show "The Good Wife", then plugs Rahm hosting lunch with labor union big shots.

* * *

Got a call from my friend Mike "Pickle" Joyce today. He asked me if I wanted to work on Chuy Garcia's mayoral campaign.

"Maybe you and Crawford could make some money."

"Yeah, how much could we make?"

Pickle explained they needed our help generally with the white ethnic wards, more specifically the Irish vote.

I was interested.

I needed dough. I always do. Who doesn't these days?

I remembered the words of my old pal Marty O'Connor, the late Chicago Daily News reporter and sometime TV political commentator. Whenever we discussed making a buck in politics, Marty always advised. "Get the money . . . everything else is nonsense."

I took it to heart. Getting the money up front always assuaged the inevitable heartbreak that was sure to come.

"Crawford" was Bill Crawford, my sometime partner in media relations capers and campaigns. Including Crawford in the deal meant I would have to get twice as much as I wanted because I'd have to split it with him. He was always a good prop to have though, because he has a Pulitzer Prize and was with the Tribune for over twenty years as an investigative reporter. That made the suckers sit up and pay attention. He was also a veteran of dozens of campaigns and we had worked at least a half dozen together chasing a buck.

Along the way we'd had lots of laughs because Bill Crawford

is a keen observer of human absurdity, which is *de rigueur* in each political campaign.

I googled Jesus "Chuy" Garcia and got a thumbnail--Cook County Commissioner, former Alderman and State Senator, ally of the late Mayor Harold Washington. He was one of a handful of mayoral candidates challenging current Mayor Rahm Emanuel. He'd been recruited to run by Chicago Teachers Union boss Karen Lewis, who had dropped out of the race when she was diagnosed with a brain tumor.

The other candidates were Alderman Bob Fioretti, Dr. Willie Wilson, and perennial candidate Dock Walls. Fioretti was an old friend and investor in a couple of my theatrical ventures.

Fioretti was probably the best of them all at articulating the Mayor's misdeeds but he wasn't going to win. He had no money, no base, and was destined to be the best man, not the groom.

And if he had no money, he couldn't pay me.

I sent Fioretti a donation for twenty-five bucks online and picked up the phone to call Crawford.

"Hey Billy, I think I got a live one."

*   *   *

I slapped some biographical material together on Crawford and me, and dressed it up as a pitch to work the campaign through the primary and get Chuy into a runoff on February 24th. We wanted five grand up front and would agree to negotiate again, once we were in the runoff.

Pickle had told me, "Call Clem Balanoff and get down to meet him today."

I called Balanoff and set up a meet at campaign headquarters for 3PM.

My lovely wife was babysitting our grandkids and had the car that day, so I arranged for Crawford to pick me up in Berwyn, where I reside high atop the fifth floor of my building, looking down on the Depot District on 32nd Street.

Yes, I am the Baron of Berwyn.

So Crawford picked me up for our 3PM appointment at their campaign headquarters on West Washington, right next to a fucking abortion clinic. Yikes.

While we were driving downtown I called Pickle on the cell and told him,

"We're gonna ask for five grand."

"They will pay it."

"Okay, are you meeting us there?"

"No, I gotta pick up Jake, (his three-year-old son) at 4PM".

"I told them you would be there!"

"I'll call him at about ten to three and cancel. You guys go down there."

"Hey what the feck, you told me to set this up!"

"I can't, it's no big deal. Schaffer will meet you there, he knows the deal."

Schaffer?

That would be David Schaffer; I'll get to him in a minute.

So Crawford parks the car over on Franklin and we walk to the campaign office. It looked like it had once been a pizza parlor or maybe a Sbarro, but now it was desks and bulletin boards and a large open area of desks with phones and laptops, an improvised campaign office in a pizza parlor. A girl intercepted us as we walked in the door, "Hi! Can I help you?"

"Uh yeah I wanna order a large sausage with anchovies . . . no ha ha, we're here to see Clem Balanoff."

She directed us to a group of tables and chairs to wait for Clem.

I had googled Clem Balanoff and got a brief history of his family: Southeast side, 10th Ward, avowed enemies of Eddie Vrdolyak, bloodlines to the steel workers union, long time activists, bomb throwers basically. Clem had served as State Rep and run against Victor Vrdolyak for Alderman before working as Chief of Staff for Cook County Clerk David Orr. He'd also been involved with the Occupy Wall Street movement while on his lunch hour from his County job.

Every time I hear that word "progressive" I cringe. It reminds me of everything I hate about the Democratic Party today. I grew up in a Democratic household on the Southside of Chicago, sure my roots were 19th Ward Irish Catholic, definitely pro-labor. Hell I'm a member of three unions myself, and my brother was the state rep of our district, but the "progressive" wing of the Democratic Party stands for abortion on demand, welfare as a way of life, and homosexual honeymoons in my book.

Today I'm an independent Republican and above all, a Catholic. Deal with it.

For the moment however, I was going to keep my mouth shut if I wanted that five grand.

So me and Crawford are sitting at the table and Clem comes over, very happy to see us, very personable, very eager to hire us it seemed to me. His phone was going off every three seconds and he was amazed at how busy he was as he told us his story. Tenth Ward renegade with his dad, years of protesting and fightin' the man, blah blah blah. You'd think we were interviewing him for the job. He was telling us his story like he was Woody Guthrie campaigning across America for the workingman, the great-unwashed public.

We schmoozed with Clem about Ed Sadlowski, a hero of the labor movement on the East Side who I had the pleasure of interviewing for the Sun-Times years ago. This is good. Ed and I had gotten along great and my column on him was a valentine and hopefully he will tell Clem I'm okay.

Andrew Sharp comes over. He's the campaign manager, introduces himself and we speak with him briefly. After Andrew walks away I ask Clem, "I thought you were the campaign manager?"

Clem scoffs and rolls his eyes, and says something like "He thinks he is."

Then the candidate, Jesus "Chuy" Garcia, comes over to us and we meet him. Immediately liked him, very engaging guy with a nice touch of self-deprecation. Talks about his neighborhood in Little Village, came to USA at the age of ten from Durango, Mexico and learned to adapt. Went to St. Rita!

Chuy leaves and I hand Clem a copy of our pitch packet. Clem is supremely confident of victory in the election, predicts a runoff and his enthusiasm is contagious.

So we're getting along great with ol' Clem and then Schaffer waltzes in the door.

David Schaffer is a Harvard educated lawyer who sees himself as a genius in training. I've known him peripherally for years. He's a former seminarian and was an acolyte of the one and only, late, (God rest his soul), Tom "Tuna" Carey. Tuna was an idiot savant in terms of campaigns and polling who I had the pleasure/pain of working with in the past. He had major health issues over the last few years but he still stood as the man who got John Stroger elected Cook County Board President in 1994. Tuna also battled for years with booze, turning him cuckoo on a regular basis, and had burnt more bridges than the St. Ben's parish pyromaniac.

Schaffer however is a position paper guy, a political guru in his own mind, a wanna-be with money, a very dangerous combination.

Schaffer is wearing his pin-striped suit under his winter parka and starts walking around like he owns the joint. We've met maybe a dozen times over the last ten years so it's not like I don't know the guy. I figure Pickle told him to come by and give us the green light. Slam-dunk.

So Crawford excuses himself to run and feed the parking meter and Schaffer picks up our pitch packet and starts reading it. I'm shootin' the biscuit with Clem about the tenth ward and Schaffer says,

"What is this?"

"Whattya mean?"

"What is this?", and he holds up the sheaf of papers promoting Crawford's Pulitzer Prize and our combined seventy-five odd years of experience in politics, journalism, show biz, and media.

He lifts up the papers like he's chastising his dog for crappin' all over them. "What is this?"

I give him the eyeball.

"Those are our bios. What the hell do you think it is?"

"Why don't you have any of the campaigns you've worked on listed here?"

You mother . . . fucker. I suddenly realized that Schaffer was sandbagging our pitch. But why? Pickle had sent him to meet us, the scene wasn't supposed to play like this. Sure, I had a list of campaigns like that,.. back home in my computer. I forgot it, but so the fuck what?

I turned to Clem. "Well, Dave, I was just about to tell Clem about those campaigns, . . . before you so conveniently tried to stab me in the back during this interview."

Schaffer mumbles something like "Well no, I was just pointing out. . . ."

I turned to Clem and started wracking my brain for campaigns we'd worked on when Crawford walked back in. I shouted at Bill as he came through the door, "Hey, what other campaigns have we worked on?"

Crawford rattles off a few and I decide to leave Schaffer out of any further discussion. I look at Clem, "I'm a George Ryan guy, one of the finest men I've ever met in politics, worked for him as Secretary of State, then Governor."

He'd also gone to jail, but I told Clem, "He was my friend and I'm also proud to say we are still friends."

I told Clem I would email him an official list of campaigns later that night. I went in for the final pitch.

"Look, ultimately the issues take a back seat to the personality of the candidate. Does the voter like the guy? You got a likeable guy who is not Rahm Emanuel, we can sell that to white ethnic voters, city workers, cops, firemen, people who work for a living. He's a St. Rita Mustang, that's a big deal, a Catholic Leaguer. We can help you win. We want five grand up front and we will negotiate again once we're in the runoff. Whaddya think?"

Clem smiles and says, "I will call you tomorrow and let you know. Thanks for coming down."

We take a brief tour of the offices and breeze out the door.

*   *   *

Walking back to Crawford's car and my blood pressure starts boiling as I think back to Schaffer sandbagging us. Crawford doesn't know what the hell I'm talking about because he was feeding the meter when Schaffer slipped the knife in.

The older I get the harder it is to come down from a rage, something happens and I just flip out, sort of like that green cartoon guy. I don't remember this happening when I was younger but maybe that's because I would just pop somebody and release the aggression, but you can't do that anymore . . . without getting arrested . . . or bloody.

I felt good about our chances of getting hired. Don't ask why, maybe the freedom of not giving a shit either way. But I really felt like we could help this guy and the more I thought about Rahm Emanuel the more I disliked him. I'd heard so many stories about what a little prick he was that I wanted to kick his ass myself.

So we're driving back in Crawford's car and I call Pickle on the cell and tell him how his pal tried to throw a monkey wrench into our gig and why would he do that? "He's got a screwy personality."

I still think we're going to get hired when I am dropped off in front of The Barony in Berwyn.

So I get home and still feel pretty good but that anger is gnawing at me. I send Clem an email with a list of campaigns and how great it was meeting him and how we're gonna get Chuy elected.

Then I send a copy to Schaffer with a sarcastic note.

Dave:

Thanks for helping out today at the meeting with Clem. I won't forget your support and kindness in a stressful situation.

Houli

I chortle to myself as the anger bubbles up again and my phone rings, it's Schaffer.

"Hey you feckin' asshole, thanks for sandbagging us today. You're lucky I didn't give you a crack right in the mouth!"

He had entered the perfect storm of my rage and I honestly don't even know why I answered the phone but there was not going to be a stop to me blowing my gasket. I was enraged, it kind of scared me actually.

To my surprise he fought back and said he was the biggest single investor on the campaign to the tune of over twenty grand and he had the power to nix my deal so I had better start . . .

I cut him off, "Oh I guess I'm supposed to kiss your ass now, huh?"

He started to calm down but I was still seething. Once I blow my gasket it's hard to keep it under control, the rage has a mind of its own. I fought with myself internally, knowing if I kept at it I could kiss my five grand goodbye.

Next thing I know Schaffer is telling me, "I'm sorry if I offended you."

Well that sounds like my out, and I said, "Okay, goodbye." Or something like that.

My wife came in the room and said, "Who were you talking to like that, using such language?"

Did it sound that bad? . . . I think I might have just shot myself in the foot.

I called Pickle.

*   *   *

Saturday, January 17- 2015.

Chicagoland

17-year-old Walter L. Wright was shot in the chest last night in Gage Park and killed. Two other young men were shot in Englewood, one is in serious condition, another shot in the face in Roseland, and a 20-year-old black male was shot in the ass in Humboldt Park.

*   *   *

The next day I start calling Clem, leaving messages cuz he never picks up his phone.

I figure Schaffer has screwed us but I also think I have nothing to lose so I'm going to rattle Clem's cage hoping to shake that five grand loose.

After a series of voice mails left on his phone, I send Clem an email.

Clem-

Here's a rundown on Irish radio in Chicago I wrote for last year's St. Pat's Parade Book. You can purchase spots on any of these shows for less than $100 per spot.

There is a huge core group that listens to all these shows. I doubt if any other candidates will be doing this, so Chuy could own Irish radio for a song!

Houli

What the hell, if I can't get the five large maybe I can at least sell them some ads on my radio show.

Still no response.

And then this via email from Clem.

Can you please write up a quick proposal with deliverables, so I can talk with others in the campaign about your services? We are a relatively poor campaign trying to go up on TV, so any diversion of dollars needs to be talked about before being spent.

Thanks.

Clem

Sounded good to me, we were still in play. I called Crawford.

They want a proposal.

"Didn't we just give them a proposal?"

Hey, it just means we refine the bullshit a bit more. I'll put together a couple pages of crap and then send it to you for your seasoned horse manure.

This is Billy Crawford's bailiwick. He is after all, a Pulitzer Prize winning journalist and he can spin with the best of them.

January 18, 2015 Sunday
Chicagoland

Cornelius Hunter, 23, and 18-year-old Bernard Pippen were both murdered last night in Chicago. Pippen was shot in the neck and Hunter in the chest. Four other males and one female were also shot and police are also investigating the death of Leona Williams in Washington Park.

*   *   *

Between us, me and Crawford came up with seven pages outlining our pure positive "plan" for victory. I won't bore you with it now but it was great bullshit.

I send it off to Clem, "looking forward to working with you guys."

January 19, 2015, Monday
Chicagoland

Shawn Holloway, 22, was murdered last night, shot in the back on the near west side. 6 other black males also shot across the city.

First thing in the morning I start calling Clem, no response.
I send him another email.

Clem

Did you get the proposal? I am on deadline for the Irish American News today/ tomorrow latest so if you want me to write a column on Chuy for the February issue I need your decision.

Please let me know.

Thanks

No response. This is a hell of a way to run a campaign, guy never returns phone calls.

Tuesday January 20, 2015

Police found the dead body of a female, severely burned in a garage fire at 60th and Campbell last night. 4 black males also shot across the city.

Call Clem again a couple three times, nothing.

Wednesday January 21, 2015

Derrick McIntyre, 26, shot and murdered last night in South Shore, and another male 16, shot in the leg in Garfield Park.

Call Clem again, nada.
He's going to miss the deadline to even get an ad in the Irish American News, my commission would be about a buck and a half. Nothing to lose and I send another email.

This is from Cliff Carlson, editor of Irish American News. If you want to take an ad you should call him today. Rate card attached. Paper hits on February 1st.

Houli

Tell em almost all of our readers are over 25 and vote!
The digital copy gets over 40,000 hits a month!
15,000 print copies average 3 to 4 readers per family!

Cliff Carlson

No reply, I'm getting frustrated by this guy so I text him.

I had to file my column, couldn't wait. You still might have time to place an ad, but must act today. Sorry we couldn't help with the campaign, good luck.

Mike Houlihan

And then around 11 AM, this.

We want to hire you. Give me a call. Clem

So I start calling the guy and can't get him on the phone. WTF! Meanwhile I got Crawford calling me every twenty minutes, "when do we get paid?"

Finally, around 4:30 that afternoon, I send another email.

That's great, I left you a couple messages but no call back.

Houli

No communication the rest of the day with this fricking guy.

Thursday January 22, 2015

Heath Huntspoon 25, shot in the chest and murdered last night, also Edwin Cook 19, killed in Chicago Lawn, and Daniel Woods, 40, shot and killed at 51ˢᵗ and Racine. 12 shot overall, with 3 murders. Also Rashan Terry, 32, shot in the head critically in Washington Park.

I'm scheduled to get two teeth pulled today and I'm driving down to the dentist at 8:30AM and Clem texts me his phone number at the campaign office.

I call Crawford and tell him to take over because I'm going to be all screwed up after the oral surgery. So he makes an appointment to meet Clem that morning.

When I come out of the surgery I text Crawford.

Clem Balanoff, 312-487-xxx0. Campaign office 312-207-xxx2. We must get check for five before starting.

Except I wrote, "musn't" instead of "must". Hey come on, I was wacked out on Novocain and had just had two molars yanked.

So I call Crawford after I have a nap and recover from my ordeal and guess what? He met with Clem, signed a contract, but did NOT get the check!

I suddenly felt like they had pulled five teeth not two.

Friday, January 23, 2015
Chicagoland

Three shootings last night in Washington Park, Roseland, and Austin.

So I wake up today feeling ready to get this guy elected. But I'm still wary without that dough.

I call the campaign office and talk to Josh Kilroy, the slug who hangs around the office and answers the phones. I met him the first day, seemed like a nice guy although he might make a better impression if he spent a little more time with the hot and soapy.

Turns out he's Schaffer's brother-in-law. That figures.

Kilroy tells me Chuy will be attending a big event Saturday night at his alma mater, St. Rita. That could be good. I look it up online and the event is the Winter Fest and they're charging fifty bucks a head. Yeah I should go, but do I risk the fifty bucks before being paid?

No, I've got a better idea.

I remember talking St. Rita Mustang football with Chuy when we had met that first day. He told me he played J-V, not varsity, "Are you kiddin', I was just a little shrimp, we had guys like Dennis Lick playing varsity for Rita then!"

Dennis Lick of course was the pride of St. Rita football, offensive lineman at Wisconsin, and Lick played six seasons with the Bears from 1976 to 1981. I had met Dennis over the holidays at Charlie Carey's Christmas party at Gene and Georgetti's. I called Charlie and he had me call our friend Tom Hicks who played on the Bears. Tommy gave me Lick's number and I called him.

I start schmoozing the great Dennis Lick and tell him, "I'm workin' for the St. Rita alum and the next mayor of Chicago, Chuy Garcia."

"Chuy is a fan of yours and I would love for you guys to have the opportunity to meet each other officially tomorrow night at St. Rita Winterfest and hopefully get a photo of you guys together."

So Lick says, "Sure, have them call me to set up the time to meet at the event!"

Yes! I call Josh the slug back and give him Dennis Lick's phone number. "I can't make it tomorrow night but he's waiting for you guys to call and coordinate the photo op."

I'm envisioning the photo plastered all over The 19th Ward with fellow St. Rita Mustangs Chuy and Dennis Lick and I'm licking my chops.

Shit they should pay us five grand just for that!

Saturday, January 24, 2015

13 shot last night including a 14-year-old girl in Austin. Abraham Burgo 35, Anfernee Durant 19, and 18-year-old Tyree Durant, all murdered.

Sunday January 25, 2015

10 people shot last night including homicide victim Arturo Olivera, 24, murdered in Garfield Park.

So I'm feeling pretty good today but still don't have that *do re mi* in the bank and the only way to get it is to go down there. I call the campaign office and Kilroy answers the phone.

"Hey Josh, how did the St. Rita alumni event go last night?"

"It went great, Chuy shook a lot of hands and got a great reception."

"Did you get the photo op with Dennis Lick?"

"Of course we did!"

Let the record show that this is the first of many lies told me on this campaign. I was on the phone so I couldn't see if that bozo had lied with a straight face but it was my first indication that something wasn't right with these "progressives". At the moment however, I believed him, I wanted to.

That's great, lemme talk to Clem.

So Clem gets on the phone and I tell him I want to pick up my check. He puts me off for today but suggests I swing by tomorrow. OKAY.

Monday, January 26, 2015

Six shot last night including a 26-year-old female shot critically in the head, and Alexander Villafane, 39, shot in the head and killed in Little Village.

I drive down to the campaign headquarters around nine am and park right in front, telling myself, "You are not leaving without that money."

I fly in the door and spy Clem sitting at his desk in the back of the office and point at him. He waves me over while on the phone and we start chatting as best we can and he introduces me to a couple of volunteers from Operation Acorn who have just started working on the campaign. These Bolsheviks looked like they had just crawled out of the commie cellar and I kept thinking of the words of Marty O'Connor, "Get the money, everything else is nonsense."

So Clem hangs up the phone and says, "Okay so we need to get that tri-fold out as soon as we can for the 19th Ward."

"That's good, Crawford's working on that. I just came by to pick up our check."

Clem points across the room at a young Latino guy and says, "That's the guy who writes the checks right there. Hey Manny."

I jump from my seat and shake Manny's hand. This is the guy I need to befriend, the guy who writes the checks! Manny Perez

"Hi Manny, just picking up our check."

Crawford had met Manny the day he didn't get the check and signed the contract and Manny had told him something like "we'll get it to you".

I explained that we required the money up front on this deal.

"How much is the check for?"

"Five grand."

"I'm not accustomed to paying people before they have done the work."

"Well we get paid up front."

Clem, God love him, pipes in, "It's okay, you can pay them."

Manny says, "This is highly irregular."

It was only tense for a minute or two but then I took out my phone and said, "Here, I'll get Bill Crawford on the phone right now, he'll explain our policy."

Manny's face is kinda turning pale as he walks back to his office and I follow him as he speaks with Crawford on the phone. He can tell that I'm not leaving and as he and Crawford talk back and forth Clem comes into the office.

I ask him, "How did it go Saturday night with Dennis Lick?"

Clem says, "Oh that didn't work out."

"Whaddya mean?"

"Well, he wasn't there or something. It went great but there was no photo with Dennis Lick"

Okay, NOW I'm getting a better idea of what we're dealing with here. I had been bullshitted on the phone by that slug Kilroy because he didn't want to deal with me. If I was going to work on a campaign with a bunch of progressive pussies who lied to each other all day I had damn well better get paid upfront.

Finally, Manny hands me back my phone and says, "I have to make the check-out to Bill Crawford."

"That's okay, that will work, I'm on my way to meet him now."

He puts the check in an envelope with Crawford's name on it and seals it. I open it in front of him to make sure it's the right amount, shake hands with Manny and Clem and leave.

I hop in my car and call Crawford.

"What the hell was that?" he says.

I tell him I'm on my way to see him and he tells me he has to meet a guy in Oak Brook at noon about his new book.

"I'll meet you there at 11:30, bring your checkbook!"

I drive to Oak Brook, meet Crawford in a restaurant, give him the check, get one from him for half and I'm on my way.

I got the money.

Marty O'Connor would be proud of me.

Tuesday, January 27, 2015
Chicagoland

Three black males shot last night, including a 15-year-old boy in Brighton Park.

Wednesday, January 28, 2015
Chicagoland

Three shot last night, one female 25, shot in the face and Angelo Porter, 18, murdered in Grand Boulevard.

Thursday January 29, 2015

Four shootings last night, two in Garfield Park, one in Woodlawn, and one in North Lawndale.

It's three days later and time to show them what they paid for with the annual St. Patrick's Day Parade corned beef and cabbage fundraiser at Plumber's Hall.

Pickle and I had arranged for Chuy to meet us there before the dinner and walk him through the crowd for an improvised meet and greet.

This was a sticky situation to say the least.

The dinner is put on by Local 130, the plumber's union and sponsors of Chicago's annual St. Pat's parade, the dying of the river green, the whole shebang in the Loop, probably one of the most political events of the year. The Plumbers had endorsed Rahm, big time, one of the first unions to back him in the first election and his heaviest labor backers.

Luckily Rahm was not going to be there that night.

But Chuy was.

I told my pal Bob Flood that Chuy Garcia was going to be joining us for the dinner that night and Flood exclaimed, "The guy from the White Sox?"

On top of the Plumbers putting the dinner on in their hall and them being Rahm's biggest supporters, they were also sponsors of the radio show I co-host every Saturday afternoon, "The Skinny & Houli Irish Hour".

It's been a tradition for at least the last five years for the Skinny & Houli Show to take a table to the fundraiser/corned beef dinner. It was always a blast and the corned beef is out of this world and every Mick on the make is in the crowd. It's one of the biggest Irish American events of the year and I was bringing the rest of our sponsors and oh yeah, mayoral candidate Commissioner Chuy Garcia.

My co-host Skinny Sheahan was still in Florida for the winter and attempting to stay out of the political fray that was about to catch fire.

The other part of this imbroglio was the check in my pocket for $850 to pay for the table. Yes, it would go towards the parade but it was still a lot of dough compared to what the plumbers paid for their advertising on the show, 75 bucks a week. It was going to take about eleven weeks to get that dough back out of them. The year before they had let me skate, just never cashed the check.

But something told me they were going to take my money this time.

So all of this is whirling around in my head as I handed over the check at the registration table that night. I'll never see that dough again I thought as I turned and walked to the parking lot to meet Chuy.

No turning back now.

The crowd hadn't hit its peak yet but still there was about five hundred in the union hall, mostly in the bar on the first floor. They would eventually ascend to the main dining room, seating about a thousand- chowing down with some beers, banners and green and white bunting everywhere.

I had scoped out the room before bringing the candidate in and had plotted taking a hard left as we circled into the bar area and work our way around the long oval bar out into the ante room with tables and chairs and then up to the second floor for a full on assault on the main dining room. Chuy had another fundraiser to hit so he was going to take an early duck, which was fine with me because I gave his ticket to Skinny's brother, Johnny Vegas the billboard king.

I shot the breeze with Judge John Griffin and pal Danny Pierce in the vestibule of the bar and nonchalantly let it drop that Chuy was on his way and would be at my table. They didn't beef, and in fact I remembered that Griffin had gone to St. Rita! Both seemed to think that Chuy had a shot at the title and I figured they would be our first stop when we wheeled Chuy into the room.

I stepped into the hallway and dialed Pickle, where the hell are you?

"I'm in traffic, here's his cell phone number, just meet him and start taking him through."

Swell.

So I grit my teeth and walk out to the parking lot. It's a brisk evening and I dial Chuy's phone. He picks up, and as we are talking I see him walking towards me. "Oh, okay I see ya."

We hang up our phones, shake hands, and head into the jaws of hell.

He's got a guy with him with a bag of buttons. "This is Jose."

Of course it is.

So we march into the bar and I grab John Griffin and Danny Pierce and, "Say hello to Chuy Garcia fellas."

That became my mantra as we swam through the crowd around the bar, lots of hard-ass union guys giving me the stare, but when I would approach and

"Hey can I introduce you guys to Commissioner Chuy Garcia?" They would melt and suddenly very friendly. Chuy was a natural, quick "hello, nice to meetcha', and I'd appreciate your support."

While I'm leading Chuy through the crowd shaking hands, I am watching the periphery of union guys reacting to the retail politics in action and I know it will only be minutes before some plumber gives us some shit. But they were gentlemen all, and what we tend to forget is that just because the union bosses back this guy Rahm, that don't mean "Joe Plumber" is down with that. As a matter of fact, we were picking up some very strong anti-Rahm vibes from these guys and many are damn friendly.

We're just making almost the complete turn around the bar and out to the next room when Mike Tierney marches up to me and says, "I need to talk to you!"

Mike is the political director for Local 130 and he looks like he's got smoke coming out of his ears he's so pissed off.

He takes me aside as Chuy schmoozes a trio of union guys at the bar and Tierney tells me, "The Plumbers are 150% behind the Mayor."

"That's great."

"So what's HE doing here?"

"He's shaking hands, meeting the voters."

"What's he doing here?"

"He's here for the corned beef and cabbage."

"Who invited him?"

"I did."

"You?"

I thought Tierney's head was gonna explode at that point. Meanwhile I'm thinking yeah I invited him to sit at the table cuz I just paid $850 bucks for that fecking table! But instead I just turned to

Chuy and his campaigning and we made our way to the other side of the room shaking hands along the way.

Finally, Pickle shows up and we take Chuy upstairs to the main dining room but it's practically empty except for the gals from Harrington's setting out the apple pie at each place setting.

Houli with Chuy
Photo courtesy of Mike Joyce.

Pickle's dad is Jeremiah Joyce, former copper, senator, and Chicago political war horse. He'd run against Mayor Daley's machine in 1975 to become Alderman of the 19th Ward, then later became a top political adviser to Richard M Daley, I'd spent a half hour talking on the phone with him a couple nights earlier as he schooled me on tactics that might help Chuy in the campaign.

The Chicago Teachers Union had called a strike in Rahm's first term and he tangled with formidable Union boss Karen Lewis who had dropped out of the mayoral race early because of a brain tumor diagnosis. Karen had urged Chuy to take on Rahm.

According to Lewis, Emanuel had taken her to dinner and was quite candid in his language and philosophy. "When I first met him, we had dinner together, and he said, "Well, you know, 25 percent of these kids are never going to be anything. They're never going to amount to anything. And I'm not throwing money at it."

His disregard for the school children incensed Lewis and she didn't hold back her contempt for that line of thinking, when Rahm told her, "Fuck you. Lewis."

Classy guy.

If Chuy could pick a moment in debate when he can recreate that story and then ask the Mayor, "What if someone spoke to your mother like that? Or your wife? Or your daughter or sister? What kind of man are you?"

I thought this would be a brilliant attack on Emanuel and while listening to Pickle give Chuy advice as we stood by the entrance to the main hall and snapped photos together I made that suggestion.

Chuy told me, "Ah, yeah I'm going to save that one for the ABC debate, more people will be watching."

But he never did say it to him.

We took him downstairs for one more run at the bar room and he left.

I could feel the daggers from the Local 130 guys across the room. They were pissed. Well time to enjoy my last meal.

I sat down with the lads way back in the corner where the Plumbers had put us and we feasted on corned beef and cabbage and beers and apple pie. I gave a sawbuck to our waiter and he gave me an extra corned beef to take home. I'd come prepared with a plastic bag in my sport coat pocket. This wasn't my first rodeo.

Our gang at the Corned Beef & Cabbage dinner.
Houli with extra corned beef to take home.
Photo courtesy of Mike Houlihan

Friday, January 30, 2015
Chicagoland

Five shot last night, including Mayron Collier 24, shot in the head and killed; Kenneth Guise 39, shot in the head and killed, and Israel C. Pena, 20, shot in the chest and killed.

Saturday, January 31, 2015
Chicagoland

Two killed last night, including Leandrew Harper, 34, shot and killed in Englewood and six-year-old Allison Lopez, a victim of child abuse.

February 1, 2015 Super Bowl Sunday
Chicagoland

Three shot last night, including the murder of Savoy Young 22, in South Chicago, and the murder of Cierra Moore, 27, who was stabbed to death in Roseland.

Our plan was to meet Chuy at Pickle's house on Sunday at 3:45. But the snow started coming down and I wanted to get ahead of it.

I drove through the falling snow to Pickle's house in Beverly. It was Super Bowl Sunday and we wanted to take Chuy to all the bars on Western Avenue and 111th Street in the 19th Ward to do some "retail" with the sports fans and introduce him to the regular guys and gals of the city.

I had called Crawford when I got home from 11AM Mass and asked him 'what time are you meeting us?'

"It's snowing and I live in Naperville!"

And I split the money with this mope.

I got to Pickle's around 1PM, the game didn't start til about 5 but we wanted to get ahead of it and the weather report was now calling it a blizzard. I knew my car would never make it, so we were going to ride in Pick's SUV. I had called Billy Guide, owner of the Cork and Kerry on Western avenue to let him know we were coming.

We got there around 3 and the joint was practically empty. The new plan had Clem picking Chuy up at his home in Little Village and because of the snow they were going to drive down Western to avoid the Dan Ryan traffic.

Turns out Brian Hickey, President of Local 399, was hosting a Super Bowl party at the Cork and he was there with his cousin Willie Winters and a few other guys. I had called the Beverly Review and Daily Southtown who both told me they would send reporters or photographers to meet us. I had talked to reporter Mike Nolan from the Southtown and photographer Vince Johnson, but then it just kept snowing.

And snowing.

We shot the breeze with a few folks in the back room. I said hello to Brian Hickey; but knew he had endorsed Rahm so he wouldn't be too happy to see our special guest. Brian shook my hand but gave me the eyeball at the same time as if to say, "What the hell are you up to now?"

Then Clem and Chuy walk in and Pickle whips out a St. Rita Mustang red hoodie sweatshirt and tells Chuy, "Put this on."

I thought that was a stroke of genius and evidently, so did Chuy because he loved it and was beaming as he modeled it for us in the back room. He did a quick interview with Kyle Garmes from the Beverly Review and by now there were only about twenty or thirty people in the bar, the game had yet to start.

Kyle got a couple photos of guys talking with Chuy for the Beverly Review, the local 19th Ward neighborhood paper and a great way to get the word out in the ward.

The snow was now coming down heavier and it was getting dark. We figured it was time to start hitting the rest of the bars.

Next stop was walking distance, Keegan's Pub, a cozy Irish joint and sometime IRA hangout. Not much action in there, maybe ten to fifteen people. I introduced Chuy to Bernard Callaghan, the owner of Keegans, "He's an immigrant, just like you!"

Bernard was gracious. As a matter of fact, everybody was. The reception was warm wherever we went. For the next several hours it was me, Chuy, Pickle, and Clem just hitting the bars and shaking hands and asking for votes.

Chuy was a regular guy and I noticed when we were talking that he didn't seem to have any accent at all, just a guy from the south side. No surprise really because he has been in Chicago since he was ten years old. But when he got nervous his accent would creep back in and make him sound somewhat wetback-ish. Or maybe that was intentional, I don't know.

I do know that he was good company.

Our goal on Super Bowl Sunday was to have Chuy meet the regular Southside folks and let them decide for themselves. He had graduated from St. Rita in 1974 and Pickle had graduated from Leo in 1986. And

I had graduated from Mt. Carmel in 1967. Okay so I'm the old guy but we three were all Catholic Leaguers and most of the people we'd be meeting were the same.

The snow kept falling and the temperature dropped but we kept going from bar to bar shaking hands, helping folks take "selfies" with Chuy and the one resounding message that came through from almost all of them was, "Anybody but Rahm!" The hate for Rahm was palpable and the vitriol poured out at each bar, and more aggressively so, as the night went on.

And that made sense, since we were dealing with people who work for a living, cops, firemen, city workers, and teachers. They're worried about their pensions and they knew Rahm was going to fuck them. Oh yes he would.

We hit over 14 bars that night, I can't even recall who was playing in the game except for a fleeting glance of Katy Perry riding a mechanical lion at half-time. And I wasn't even drinking! I think I had my first beer in a joint on 111th Street where the gang invited us to eat: subs and pizza and stuff brought from home and put out on the table for all.

Over and over again we heard, "You came out on a night like this to hear what we have to say? You got my vote!"

As we drove from bar to bar, Chuy brought up the story of Los San Patricio's battalion in the Mexican American War.

The San Patricios battalion were Irish immigrants who had been conscripted into the American army to fight the Mexicans. But the Irish guys soon discovered that the mostly Protestant army officers treated the Catholics like crap, in fact were openly hostile to the Catholic soldiers and they began to wonder why they were fighting against the Mexicans, also Catholics. A guy named John Reilly got a group of them together and they joined the other side, fighting for Mexico.

The Irish soldiers won a battle or two and went down in history as the Saint Patrick's battalion.

Most of them were also later executed, but we didn't get into that.

So we were talking to Chuy about this and there we were, the Irish guys helping a Mexican guy run for Mayor. And a St. Rita guy to boot. And that is how we bonded that night of the Super Bowl.

Our last stop was my favorite watering hole on the Southside, Ken's at 105th and Western. As we were walking in I told Chuy, "This is my favorite bar."

When he asked me why, I told him, "Because I never have to pay for a drink!"

So we're sitting in a booth in Ken's with Frankie Moran and retired Fire Commissioner Jim Joyce and they're talking pension deals with Chuy and I tell these guys I have an idea for a new slogan. "Vote for Chuy, the honorable hombre!"

Chuy says, "I like that."

And then I tell him, "Ya'know what Rahm's campaign slogan should be? 'BOHICA, Bend Over, Here it Comes Again!'"

Monday, February 2, 2015

Two shootings last night and one murder of Antonio Gamboa, 23, who was stabbed to death at 23rd and Michigan.

FREE CRAIC Citizens Report American Irish Culture

The Chuy Garcia 19th Ward Super Bowl Blitz

Posted on February 2, 2015 by Mike Houlihan

Mayoral Candidate Jesus "Chuy" Garcia is a proud
St. Rita Mustang.

The gang at TR's in Mount Greenwood welcome Chuy to
their neighborhood.

Mayoral candidate Jesus "Chuy" Garcia plowed through the 5th largest blizzard in Chicago history to introduce himself to the Irish American community in a Super Bowl Sunday blitz of 19th Ward pubs yesterday. Decked out in the colors of his alma mater, The St. Rita Mustangs, Chuy started shaking hands in The Cork & Kerry around 3 PM and hit Keegan's, Dingers, The Dubliner, O'Brien's, O'Rourke's Office, McNally's, The Beverly Woods, Cullinan's Stadium Club, Hippo's, Galloway's Mystic Lounge, Baracco's, and TR's on 111th Street until winding up at Ken's back on Western Ave around 9PM.

The assorted Chicago Public School teachers, firefighters, police, and city workers who were hunkered down in the pubs watching the Super Bowl warmly welcomed Garcia. Many were astounded that he had come out on a night not fit for man nor beast to say hello and listen to their concerns for the city.

Garcia is now the acknowledged most dangerous challenger to Rahm Emmanuel and his millions in campaign cash. Last Wednesday, Tribune columnist, John Kass said, "In this campaign, Garcia is the neighborhood guy. And Rahm is the crafty servant of the oligarchs who own this city . . . And it appears to me that Rahm may just be a tad worried about Chuy."

The hate for Rahm in the 19th Ward was palpable on Super Bowl Sunday as one after another voter met Garcia's handshake with expletive laced pronouncements of "Anybody but Rahm". And, after brief discussions with Chuy, many enthusiastically offered atta boys in his direction.

Longtime city worker Cooder McCooder, sitting at the bar in Ken's said, "I had no idea Chuy went to St. Rita. He's a Catholic Leaguer who raised his kids in Little Village in Epiphany parish. I can vote for that all day long. Hell he's been an Alderman, State Senator, and Cook County Commissioner, I'll take that over the nine-fingered ballerina any day!"

Many city workers refer to Emmanuel with disdain as "the nine-fingered ballerina" because of his missing digit and history as a ballet dancer in college.

Emmanuel must get 50% of the vote plus one or else stand for election again in a runoff with whoever comes in second. Right now that looks to be Jesus "Chuy"Garcia. Once that happens, all bets are off. There are a lot of votes in the 19th Ward.

Copyright © 2015 FREE CRAIC

Thursday February 12, 2015

Two shootings last night, one in West Pullman and the other in Hermosa.

Father Pfleger endorses Rahm Emanuel.

What's the deal?

What kind of deal did Father Michael Pfleger cut with Mayor Rahm Emanuel for his endorsement?

Nobody endorses Rahm without a promissory note.

Magic Johnson got an $80 million contract from Rahm for his $250,000 contribution and plenty of media face time with the big, black, basketball legend. Not a bad deal for either of them, especially considering the $80 large is coming out of the taxpayers' pocket to extend Magic's janitorial company's contract to continue keeping the Chicago Public Schools so bright and clean. Yeah, right, that must be why teachers and principals have been bringing brooms from home to clean up the filthy condition they work in.

It looks like a smart business decision for Magic.

But what about you, Father Mike? What do you get?

How do you go to your St. Sabina parishioners with a straight face and tell them "Rahm is cool" when he has presided over an unprecedented four years of violence in the black community, practically wiping out a generation of young African American men?

What do you tell the mothers of those kids who believed Rahm really would hire more cops, and then didn't, and then their sons were murdered on the streets of Rahm's Chicago?

And what is a Roman Catholic pastor doing, making political endorsements? Where is the new Cardinal on this deal with the devil?

What about the words of Chicago Teachers Union President Karen Lewis when she spoke of Rahm Emanuel? "When I first met him, we had dinner together, and he said, "Well, you know, 25 percent of these kids are never going to be anything. They're never going to amount to anything. And I'm not throwing money at it."

That was Rahm talking about some of the kids from your parish Father Mike.

St. Sabina was established in 1916 to serve a primarily Irish congregation. Today this Gothic-style church is a self-sufficient, thriving African American Catholic community that boasts 2,000 members and a school of 500 students in grades kindergarten through eight.

If you had pulled a stunt like this back in 1916 with your Irish parishioners, they would have thrown you out in the street. Why won't they do it now? What were you promised Father Michael Pfleger?

Have you surrendered your immortal soul?

Did you make a deal with the devil, Father Pfleger?

Southside Jimmy Goff once told me:

"Pfleger has such low regard for black people that he thinks they'll fall for the okey-doke everytime. He probably has that Munchausen syndrome; he just likes publicity for publicity sake. If you told him, 'Put on a pair of ladies underwear and we'll put you on Time magazine', he'd do it in a second".

February 16, 2015
Chicagoland

Lynell Bradley Jr., 37, was gunned down last night in Englewood.

So two weeks have gone by since our Super Bowl whirlwind and I'm starting to feel guilty. Crawford has worked up three different variations of a Southside mailing piece trifold and I've been tinkering with a mailer that lists 5 THINGS YOU DON'T KNOW ABOUT CHUY GARCIA.

But unfortunately nobody from the campaign returns phone calls or delivers orders or anything. Just radio silence. I'm starting to wonder whose side these fakers are on!

The Portage Park Neighborhood Association (PPNA) will host a Mayoral Candidates' Forum in the 658-seat Auditorium of the Irish American Heritage Center, located at 4626 North Knox Avenue, Chicago, on Monday, February 16th, 2015 from 7pm-9pm. Admission is free and seating is on a first come, first served basis.

The four challenging candidates; Bob Fioretti, Jesus Garcia, William Walls and Willie Wilson are confirmed to attend. Mayor Rahm Emanuel has been invited, but is unconfirmed. The Mayoral Election is Tuesday, February 24.

Tonight Chuy is set to appear at the Irish American Heritage Center for a Mayoral Forum with all the candidates. Not really a debate, they each take turns talking with a moderator onstage. Rahm stiffs it.

I figure it would be a good idea to show my face, fly the flag, so to speak.

I know just about everybody at the Heritage Center, it's sort of my turf, being a columnist for the Irish paper and all.

I call Crawford, he's not going.

So I pull my ass together and get in the car and drive up there. It's a dark Monday night in the middle of winter and you could shoot a cannon off in the joint. I walk in and see just a couple guys at the bar, walk around to enter the auditorium and bump into Frank Avila.

Frank's old man is Frank Sr. a longtime Metropolitan Water Reclamation Commissioner. His wife is Sherry and she's Irish and Frank is Mexican, and they are big supporters of the Irish American Heritage Center. Their son Frank is a very colorful character in his own right, retired Army officer, attorney, sometime candidate, and consistent political advisor.

Full disclosure, I appeared with my sons on Frank's Cable Access

TV Show, "Magnificent Obsessions" and we talked up our indie feature film, "Tapioca".

We looked at the tape online a couple months later and all agreed that we looked like idiots. But, that's show biz.

Frank grabs me and introduces me to candidate Willie Wilson, sort of a black preacher type.

Willie Wilson is a rag to riches success story who is also a candidate for Mayor. He has a very eccentric style of talking . . . in that you usually can't understand a frickin' word he is saying.

It's Jive!

He is also looking to knock Rahm off his throne, so that's cool. My enemy's enemy is my friend.

It's also rumored that Mr. Pickle Joyce is advising Willie Wilson on his campaign as well. There's some labyrinthine logic to that, which Pickle once explained to me, but for the life of me I can't recall why he was a close confidant to Willie, but he was.

Pickle tells me later: *"I helped him early on because I had a relationship with him through the black community, where he is a philanthropist. Willie Wilson, as an African American, was bringing up relevant issues which resonated in the Black community. We needed Willie's help in the run-off."*

There could be no run-off without Willie Wilson.

Frank Avila was also helping Rev. Willie Wilson, and helped get him on the ballot.

Willie's wearing a neon green tie that he bought in the gift shop of the Heritage Center and Frank gives me the big buildup.

Dr. Willie Wilson at IAHC.
Photo courtesy of Mike Houlihan.

"Hey Houli, have you met Dr. Willie Wilson?"

"Hiya Willie, good luck in the election!"

I walk into the auditorium and there's only about 50 people sitting there listening to the moderator talking onstage with Dock Walls.

The thing about Dock Walls is he makes sense, makes a great argument for his candidacy but has run for just about every office under the sun in the last decade. He's going nowhere.

I blow out into the hallway and grab a Guinness at the bar in a plastic cup. Nosing around the hallway I look in a classroom and see Fioretti being coached by somebody I can't see, looks like he's waiting to go on. I catch his eye and he gives me the nod, through the glass of the door, probably heard I'm working for Chuy so he doesn't bother getting up, just the nod.

Sorry Bob, but you got no money and no base and you aren't gonna win. And if you got no money how could you pay me? He probably forgot the 25 bucks I sent online before I started on this race.

Moseying down the hall now I'm reminding myself to stay away from that part of the corridor, don't really want to talk to him other than wish him well.

I walk back towards the auditorium and who should I bump into but Chuy and Manny just offstage. Hey boys.

Shakes are exchanged and Chuy eyes my Guinness and says, "Looks like YOU'RE doin' good."

He's on next so I wish him luck. Not really worried about the booze glance, it's not like they've been asking for my help and I am, after all, on my own turf, so chill Chuy.

I grab a seat in the auditorium and watch Chuy as he's being questioned by the moderator.

Chuy gives his stump intro and opens with something like "My name is Chuy Garcia and yes I am a politician." It's a refreshing bit of honesty but the rest of his appearance is ruined by the moderator doing his best PBS imitation of Charlie Rose and making me very bored.

I slink out of the auditorium and back to the bar. There I run into Schaffer, who is now my buddy, ha ha. He points out a reporter from the Washington Post on the other side of the Fifth Province Pub and I walk over and introduce myself. The guy's name is Sean Sullivan and he's in town for the week to do stories on the mayoral race in Chicago.

He starts making all these allusions to Chuy being the next Elizabeth Warren or Bill DeBlasio. WTF? I tell him Chuy is a just a guy from St. Rita from the old neighborhood. He has no clue what I'm talking about and once again I'm bored by some progressive numb-nuts trying to impress me. I get back to my seat at the bar next to Schaffer and Chuy and Manny come in.

Chuy buys me a pint. Good man.

Schaffer says to Chuy, "You should talk to Mike about all his experiences on other campaign trails."

I can't tell if he's being a wiseass or just patronizing, but I remember

I've already been paid so I've got nothing to lose when Chuy asks me what I thought of his new TV commercial.

I hated it, thought it was total dogshit. It was Chuy standing on a porch in his overcoat looking into the camera/teleprompter reading some bullshit about what I can't remember. Supposedly Don Rose put it together and it is cinematically forgettable.

I tell Chuy, "Yeah I saw it, I didn't like it."

Chuy looks surprised, "Why didn't you like it?"

Because the evil little weasel on everybody's mind was never mentioned in the commercial, Rahm. The candidate with all the money. The incumbent. And Chuy's guys use what little money they have to perch him on a porch in front of a teleprompter and yes, talking with the accent, making him sound like he got to Chicago ten minutes ago.

I tell Chuy, "I don't know man, I guess it's not your fault, maybe it's not in your nature, but you've gotta kick this guy in the balls!"

Chuy smiles and takes a sip of his Guinness, "Kick . . . him . . . in the balls?"

"Yeah this is a street fight man, come on, you're from the south side, you know what I'm talking about, the only way to win this is to kick him directly in the balls, repeatedly."

I tell Chuy he's gotta take it to Rahm and Frank Avila walks up with the black overcoat collar up and a beer in his hand, he looks like a scene out of ON THE WATERFRONT and I ask Chuy,

"Do you know Frank Avila?"

They both laugh and sort of begrudgingly acknowledge that they have known each other for a long, long time. These are two of the gladiators who have worked in the Coliseum's lobby for years and are now itching to get out there in the center ring.

We're talkin' endorsements and I ask Chuy,

"Did Toni Preckwinkle endorse you?"

He gave me a sheepish look and shook his head NO.

"I thought you were her guy?"

Chuy was the floor leader on the county board for Preckwinkle but something about Rahm scared her. She would have been delighted to see Chuy upend Rahm but she was not about to say it out loud. There was a lot of that going on during the campaign.

While she never endorsed Chuy she did send the great Irishman Cyril Regan from Roscommon to help out on the campaign. More on Cyril later but he is a mighty campaign advisor and advance man.

Business bearded Mike Flannery from Fox 32 News slithers through the bar now and makes some crack to Chuy about, "Watch out for these guys, Commissioner!"

Flannery lives in Beverly and he's the Chet Coppock of Chicago politics. I was attending the trial of George Ryan one day years ago with my old pal Pete Nolan and Flannery sez to me outside the court room, "What are you doing here?"

"I'm here to support my friend George Ryan. I'm gonna say a prayer for him."

"He's gonna need it!"

This douchebag had him convicted before the trial even started, another example of Chicago's media weenies. Goo-goo reporters and columnists who pretend it's all on the square, when in reality we all know that nothin's on the square.

February 17, 2015
Chicagoland

Four shootings last night, including a 12-year-old girl shot in the back at 18th and Leavitt in serious condition; and one homicide, Kristopher Claybon, shot and murdered at 57th and Hermitage.

Obama was coming to Chicago later this week to endorse the nine fingered ballerina for Mayor of Chicago. They'd be dedicating the Pullman Project in Roseland, and trying to put Rahm over the goal line. Comrades in evil, they had hijacked the project Bob Fioretti had dedicated most of his political life making happen. Fioretti grew up in Roseland, went to Mendel and started his activism helping, living, and promoting Pullman. And those bastards locked him out on the big day. All the media would attend to fawn over these two oily politicians as they pandered to the poor for votes.

Pickle called me today and we commiserated on what a puke fest that was going to be when Obama comes to town to have Rahm blow him.

"Houli we gotta do something, have a Chuy rally the same night in Beverly."

Great idea.

We chose Thursday night and thought about doing it at McNally's on Western, just past 111th Street.

That idea was scratched when we remembered that some black guy in a band had some bullshit beef with the crowd there and turned it into a media event about south side racism, all of it horseshit by the way.

So it was agreed the media would claim we are all racists if we had the meeting at McNally's.

And they would, so we switched the event to O'Rourke's Office at 111th and Western. We had two days to get the word out in the 19th Ward that we'd be having our own rally for Chuy while Rahm massaged Obama's adam's apple in Pullman.

I sent out an email blast to my radio listeners list promoting the "meet Chuy" rally for that Thursday night at O'Rourkes. I've got a lot of names on that list and it's a good way to spread the word on short notice.

I also started calling all my pals on the Southside trying to get them to show up. I don't think we were even charging anything to get in so we had a shot.

Except that the temperature was plunging and it was gonna be freezing out.

Wednesday February 18, 2016
ASH WEDNESDAY

Two shootings last night, as well as the discovery of the dead body of Michael Franklin, 49, in a garage at 71st and Champlain.

Chuy leaving St. Peter's Catholic Church
in The Loop after receiving his ashes.
Photo courtesy of Carolina Sanchez

Thursday Feb. 19, 2015
Chicagoland

neighborhood to talk about more cops being hired, protecting your neighborhoods and your families.

DUMP RAHM

19th Warders concerned about your pensions?

THEN

Join us this Thursday night, Feb. 19th at O'Rourke's Office 11064 South Western Ave 6-8:30PM

&

Have a beer with Chuy Garcia

Rahm Emmanuel

(AP Photo/J. Scott Applewhite)(Credit: Associated Press)

Okay, obviously I was targeting the Rahm haters with this, trying to get them to come out tonight for the meet and greet at O'Rourke's. Unfortunately, my email blast hit upwards of 2500 people and not all of them share my political agenda.

Of course, by now I'd removed the guys in the Plumber's union and Fioretti himself from the database, no point rubbing their noses in it.

But evidently, I hit a nerve with some of the goo-goo members of my mailing list. Keep in mind this is MY list, although I do use it to promote my radio show. My co-host on the radio is not involved on this campaign and remains in Florida for the winter. But he got some phone calls about this email blast, oh yes he did.

So I get an email back from the late Paul Green of the City Club of Chicago. This guy was the "professor" of political science at Roosevelt University and acted as a moderator for the luncheons at the City Club. Evidently he was a fan of Rahm's. He was upset at the tone of my email and seemed to think I owe Rahm for something.

Do you guys know what you are doing? Why so anti-Rahm? Remember last year's plunge!

Paul Green

So Paul wrongly assumed that Skinny is involved with this and wanted to remind me/Skinny that Rahm Emanuel did a very successful Polar Plunge last March with Jimmy Fallon and helped raise a lot of money for Special Olympics, a charity very dear to Skinny's heart.

So I wrote back:

Paul, Skinny has nothing to do with this. I'm helping out a friend. Rahm is a bully and I don't like bullies.

Houli

I think that's about the time Paul called Skinny in Florida. And then wrote back to me.

Mike

Good luck with Skinny

Paul

Well it's not five minutes before my phone rings and it's my old pal Skinny Sheahan, and he's incensed.

"What the hell are you doing? You can't call those people fascists!!!"

"Did Paul Green call you?"

He denies that and continues to castigate me while I laugh. Evidently I had struck a nerve with "non-partisan" moderator Paul Green of The City Club of Chicago.

I tell Skinny, "They ARE fascists!" And hang up the phone.

The temperature continued to drop and by the time I got to O'Rourke's that night it was eight below zero.

I walk in the bar and there's about twenty guys in there, including Pickle, his brother, and a few of the boxers from The Celtic Boxing Club.

Stragglers stream in but I can see it's going to be a bust. Finally, Chuy comes in with Clem and Manny.

We mingle the best we can, folks want photos with Chuy.

Later that night when I'm leaving I remember Skinny telling me "you don't know what these people are like" and I get really paranoid. I had like only one beer but I purposely drove home up Western rather than the expressway in case some of Rahm's "fascist" operatives were tailing me and hoped to catch me on a DUI after the meet and greet.

Out of all the pals I texted to be there only two showed up, Frank "The Hammer" Hamer and John "Spellbound" Spellman. And they both showed up after Chuy had left.

I did get one good joke out of the night that Spellbound told us.

Guy goes to the doctor, "Doc you gotta help me, I'm having anxiety attacks, I can't get this song outta my head!"

Doc sez, "What't the song?

"What's New Pussycat!"

Doc sez "Hmmmm, sounds like you've got Tom Jones syndrome."

"Tom Jones syndrome? What the heck is that? Is it something rare?"

Doc sez, "It's Not Unusual!"

Wednesday February 18, 2015
Chicagoland

Dead body of David Moncada found in Eckart Park, 1330 West Chicago, this morning at 8:30AM. Autopsy inconclusive.

Thursday February 19, 2015
Chicagoland

Two shootings today and the murder of Julio Ramos, 31, shot in the head in Logan Square.

Saturday February 21, 2015
Chicagoland

Six shootings last night, including the gunshot murder of Malcolm Tompkins in Englewood.

South Side Irish Parade Fundraiser

Bourbon Street in Merrionette Park on 115th and Kedzie, the place is packed. I park my car over by the Jewel as I do every time I visit this joint. Made the mistake of using the valet park once back in 2003 and I waited til 2005 for the guy to go get my car. No thanks.

Pickle picks me up at my car. He has a green felt Fedora sitting on his front seat. "What the hell is that?"

"It's for Willie Wilson, I told him I would bring it."

Chuy is at another fundraiser and won't be here for about an hour but Pickle has already coordinated with Dr. Willie to do a walk-through of the crowd before Chuy gets here. We go in and I pay. Hey, gotta support the parade.

The Southside Parade was canceled a few years ago by goo-goo's on the committee who felt the drinking was getting out of control. It was resurrected by a radio talk show host by the name of Skinny Sheahan who pledged "family values' for the new parade. His nephew-in-law Alderman Matt O'Shea then did an about face and opposed the return of the parade, kissing up to Rahm. Common sense prevailed and here we are.

Dr. Willie Wilson arrives and he's wearing a dark green suit that will perfectly match the Chapeau Pickle has brought. The Doctor puts on the hat and looks like a 63rd Street pimp as Pickle leads him through the crowd shaking hands and the place goes nuts, everybody wants to pose for a selfie with Dr. Willie. He is loving it and I take a turn through the maze of micks and find myself at the end of the bar in the south corner of the gigantic hall.

I order a beer and look out at the sea of humanity. It's a great turnout and everybody seems thrilled that the parade is back to stay, thanks be to God.

I look over and see Local 130 Plumbers Union Business Manager Jimmy Coyne at the bar kitty corner from me. I wave. He smiles.

I push my way through the crowd to greet him.

"Are you mad at me?"

"For what?"

"Well, I'm with Chuy."

"Hey come on, this is America."

No Jimmy, this is Chicago . . . and we both know it. Regardless of his magnanimous manner I could tell he would love to see me disappear and I decide to do just that and make my way back to the front door to meet Chuy.

I run into Mark Sulski and his son in front of the registration table, shooting the biscuit and out comes Pickle and Willie after a sumptuous swim in the adoring crowd of folks who love Willie. Are they laughing with him or at him? He doesn't seem to care.

I gotta get a picture of this just for posterity.

Dr. Willie Wilson with Mike "Pickle Joyce,
photo courtesy of Mike Houlihan.

Willie leaves with his entourage of none, takes Pickle's hat with him.

Chuy enters, with his family and some friends.

It's Chuy, his wife Evelyn, Manny, Clem and a few others in his posse. Pickle and I greet him and dive into the crowd, tapping everybody in front of us, "Hi say hello to the next Mayor of the city of Chicago, Chuy Garcia!"

The crowd went wild. I'll bet Chuy was in a hundred selfies with Southsiders in just the first 15 minutes. He was good at it too, genuine. We met families all together and a man in his 90's in a wheel chair shook his hand. Chuy dropped to his knee and whispered in the old timer's ear. The noise in the hall was deafening Irish rock but I could see the look of appreciation in your aul one's' eyes.

The place was packed and we were just wading through the mass of humanity, everybody wanted to meet our guy. Except of course Brian Hickey, Local 399 boss who once again looked at me like I had rabies.

Clem would take the photos of folks with Chuy, and hand them back their phones, finally found his calling.

Southsiders that night felt something. Most of them Irish, on the brink of celebrating their biggest day of the year, which has just recently been resurrected after a couple years of hooliganism. There had been bad blood over the parade, many felt the rush to judgement by the city and the parade committee itself to cancel it after 35 years of tradition was bogus. Rahm was Mayor during the ban and Matt O'Shea, their own 19th Ward Alderman, had condemned the parade as out of control. He was of course currying favor with the new Mayor; but in the 19th Ward, ass kissing is considered contemptuous.

O'Shea finally got on board with the triumphant return of the parade when his uncle-in-law, Skinny Sheahan, rallied City Hall behind it. But residual resentment for Rahm still lingers. After so many years of the Irish holding the mayoral seat there weren't a lot of Southside Irish embracing this cocky shmuck from the North Shore running their city.

They saw a shot at redemption with Chuy, a St. Rita guy, sure he was a Mexican with a moustache, but tonight . . . he was our Mexican with a moustache. The crowd embraced him and Chuy felt the love. We all did.

We took a break after about a half hour and sneaked into a darkened side bar where Chuy asked for a cold beer. It was me and Pickle, Clem, Manny, Chuy's wife Evelyn, and a few loyal retainers standing in the darkness that night and all of us just catching our breath.

We could hear the roar of the crowd from the other room and Chuy chugged his beer, wiped his brow, and said, "Let's do it again!"

And so we did, the crowd parting like the red sea for their new savior.

Three days til Election Day.

Sunday February 22, 2015
Chicagoland

John Kass writes great column today in The Tribune, headline reads: **Do Chicago a favor, don't let Rahm win Tuesday,** *basically exhorts the voters to force Rahm into a runoff.*

Today was also the confrontation between Mayor Rahm Emanuel and Chicago Fire Department EMS Field Chief Patrick Fitzmaurice. It happened in a firehouse on Pulaski and North Avenue.

CFD EMS Field Chief Patrick Fitzmaurice with Houli.
Photo courtesy of Mike Houlihan.

Pat is a controversial character and has nine ambulances under his direct command. He was thrust into the public eye at a press conference, where he endorsed Chuy on January 14th. He's a tough, no-nonsense Irishman who has seen it all over the course of his 43 years with the CFD.

Pat tells me he "grew up around Grand Avenue and Cicero . . . went to Saint Peter Canisius and went to Foreman High School, although they called it ThreeMen until I got there!"

Even though Local 2 Firefighters endorsed Rahm, Pat Fitzmaurice and a hundred of his paramedic pals, started a PAC fund and, after being rebuffed by Rahm, met with Chuy, liked what they heard, and handed him a check for five grand and endorsed him at the press conference. That's when the shit hit the fan.

Fitzmaurice was candid at that press conference, telling the media that, although you may cover the murders and shootings, EMS is there on the streets every night, up close and personal, hand in hand with the dying and dead teenagers, their mothers and fathers, as they work to try and save their lives. "We know you guys cover the shootings . . . (but) we do the shootings, we're looking in their eyes, we're the ones covered with these kids' blood. This has gotta end!"

Pat was such a dynamic and effective spokesman for the paramedics and his calling out of Rahm so intrepid, that the Chuy campaign asked him, "Would you go on camera and say that?"

Fitzmaurice told me, "I said sure, why not? I don't care. And they said, think about it. And I go, 'I got nothin' to think about, what is he gonna do to me?"

I told Pat, "You know he has a history of just fecking people over?"

He laughs, "*Oh yeah, sure . . . , he acts like a tough guy, but I'm not convinced...ya make noise, that's all you do, ya make noise, ya gotta lotta money ya'know, you bully people, just cuz you can stand in front of some fat old congressman with . . . with your pants off, and threaten 'em?, pull that on me man, I'll break your ribs, gimme a break.*"

"*So I did the commercial*".

Patrick Fitzmaurice did three commercials altogether, and they are still up online on You Tube if you google them, each is a classic of a Chicago guy from the neighborhood telling it like it is about Rahm Emmanuel.

They were never broadcast, probably because of their length and the lack of money for a media buy. The first spot was titled, "The Neighborhood that God and Politics Forgot" and was released online on January 22nd. The second shorter spot was "A Pension is a Promise", released February 3rd. And finally "Solving the Problems that Rahm Created" was released March 12th. If those spots had aired on broadcast TV, we'd have a different mayor today.

Yeah, and if the dog hadn't stopped to shit, he'd have caught the rabbit.

The commercials went viral, shared on social media, on Facebook and among a variety of groups that were outraged by Rahm.

Pat Fitzmaurice was now recognizable as a guy standing up to the bully. Retribution could be swift, but it would also be almost too obvious. Pat's bravado was also his protection.

And then on Sunday word spread that Rahm was campaigning at firehouses.

It was the weekend before the first election, and we were all laughing... I mean how desperate are you, you're going to firehouses? Whattya gonna go . . . get ten votes?"

Rahm was reaching out to the ranks, trying to be a regular guy, but his proclivity for ball busting could not mask his ever present arrogance.

"But he was the same old self, he goes in there . . . The one firehouse, and he tells 'em, "I see a lot of nice cars out there",

"Oh really, is there a problem with us driving a nice car, it's only for you Rahm? Hey I'm sorry mister mayor."

CFD Field Chief Pat Fitzmaurice was working that day, making his rounds, picking up paperwork. He walked into the firehouse at Pulaski and North Avenue and the Mayor was there giving a speech. Maybe Rahm chose that firehouse because he knew Fitz worked there, wanted to confront him after all the shit he talked on camera about him. Who knows?

But Pat was just doing his job.

"And I'm like . . . oh this is beautiful, so I go down and get my paperwork and I come out and I stand and he's staring at me.

He recognized you obviously

Oh right away, and one of the firemen goes, man if looks could kill Pat, you were dead.

He got done talking to 'em, in his arrogant way, and he walked up to me . . . and he shook my hand . . . he TOOK my hand, I offered it up, he took it and he got right in my face, staring at me, and he goes, so how are YOU doing? And I remember it was a "how are YOU doing?"

It was an awkward situation at best. The Mayor confronts you where you work because you've done some negative TV spots against him. If he was looking for a fight, it would've been a short one. Rahm's security detail was waiting outside while Rahm got in Pat's face.

And I'm goin' . . . I'm doing fine, man, what're you doing? I'm standing there laughing at him, and he won't let go of my hand . . . and I'm lookin' at him. And I'm lookin' at him . . . and I wanted to say, ya'know, if you blink, you blow? Is that's what's going on here, you know cuz I'm not blinking, and your security teams out there, ya little runt, I couldn't believe it, and then he let go and he walked out.

Once back outside the Mayor got in his vehicle and picked up the phone.

Pat stood there thinking about what just happened and then his phone rang. It wasn't Rahm, it was CFD brass calling him.

And within minutes I know, one of my bosses got a call. And I'm like, yeah I went in to get my paperwork, when I walked out what was I gonna do?...Supposed to walk out on him, and the Mayor's in here talking? I can't just walk out. I didn't confront him, he confronted me. And that was it.

Monday February 23, 2015
Chicagoland

5 shootings yesterday, including the murder of Swan Lockhart, 25, in Englewood.

Tuesday Feb. 24, 2015, Election Day
Chicagoland

No reported shootings today!!!

I went to mass at 8AM at St. Odilo's in Berwyn and prayed for Chuy. Sent him a text.

"Just came from morning mass and communion, praying for your success, see you tonight.".

"God bless you Houli".

"And you pal, your cause is just, you are the right man at the right moment. So proud to be in your corner".

Pickle had started the day with Clem and Chuy out at St. Cajetan's, the local polling place in the 19th Ward.

Watched the news throughout the day and talked with Crawford about going to the party at Alhambra Palace on West Randolph. I picked up Crawford in front of the Billy Goat around 6PM and we drove over and parked in the West Loop. The joint was a huge banquet hall with stage and dance floor and rooms upstairs for private parties.

When Crawford and I got there it was almost empty, maybe fifty folks at the most. But it was still early and it promised to be a long night.

We grabbed a table and ordered some beers, casing the joint. People starting drifting in. Pickle walked in with Chuckie B. and his pal Tim Bobik. Pickle always seems to arrive with a pair of big palookas who look like they will beat the shit out of you at his command. Turns out they're great guys but what did I know? We follow them upstairs to a room in the back where the campaign has set up a bank of laptops and returns coming in. Josh Kilroy sits at the end of the table and I look over his shoulder. Nobody says hello to us.

Clem is huddled with a few others and I see Manny in passing, and tell him, 'We're going to push this to a runoff.' He fist bumps me, and there is an air of anticipation in the room. All of us thinking, this could be good, we could make history. **A runoff is unprecedented in the history of Chicago mayoral elections.**

We head over the bar adjacent to the back room and discover to my dismay that it is a cash bar. WTF? Taking this as a bad omen, Crawford and I return downstairs to the main dance floor to discuss the night before us. Pickle leaves his credit card with us and starts running a tab, that's more like it.

So me and Crawford are sitting at one of the banquettes, there's some food laid out on a table but I'm too nervous to eat, and for me that's unusual. But there was something going on, we could feel it, an electricity in the air, we started to feel that, maybe, tonight, we could show these feckers at the Sun-Times and Chicago media, that they had it all wrong. You mopes don't get it, Rahm is evil . . . and this city was going to slap him around a bit. Please God.

A huge guy with a red beard shows up and sits at our table. Jack Haines! Jack is an old school left winger from the Harold Washington days. He introduces himself, and oh yeah, we're friends on Facebook. I'd been reading his daily slams at Rahm and enjoying them, actually Facebook was a great seat for this campaign, and all the negativity was out there. Lots of folks were scared of Rahm, word on the street was he would find a way to make your life miserable if you refused to genuflect.

But on Facebook he was called every name in the book and great photos would pop up. They are all photo shopped, but that doesn't make them any less hilarious, however trying to secure the rights of these outstanding photos is impossible. But google them because you won't be disappointed.

Anyway, Jack Haines is my friend on Facebook and he sits down and he orders a drink. He's very friendly and proceeds to tell some great stories of old battles in Chicago politics. He also told us that night that he might be, just might be, the illegitimate son of Red Skelton. Lord knows he looked like Red. Jack was sort of a Clem Kaddiddlehopper lefty. We exchanged gossip throughout the night, all of us hoping and praying for a Chuy challenge to the nine-fingered ballerina.

The joint was filling up fast and characters from all over the city were streaming in the doors. Once word got out that it looked like we might be pushing Rahm into a runoff, you could feel the vibe in the room, everybody in Chicago started showing up.

The room became electric with hope. Speakers started showing up at the podium and testifying. I didn't know any of them, but Jack Haines had a rundown on all of them, mostly civil rights types, dyed in the wool goo-goo Generals.

Pickle comes back downstairs and joins us and tells us it looks good. He's got numbers but at that point I'm just buzzed and excited. Fast forward through the night of speeches and precinct reports and then it's official, there are plenty of big screen tvs in the room and everybody is watching. Congressman Luis Gutierrez comes on the screen doing an interview with CNN or somebody and the crowd goes nuts, throwing epithets and shouting out in Spanish, *traidor!*

They told me later it means "traitor" and I had to agree. His face had ignited the crowd in a pissed-off chant. It might as well have meant "cocksucker"! That little worm had endorsed Rahm over fellow Latino Chuy Garcia. Gutierrez is Puerto Rican. Historically bad blood between Mexicans and Puerto Ricans, and tonight they would have skinned him alive if he was in the room.

The crowd is going nuts, balloons, confetti, the whole bit and I run onto the dance floor to try and take a selfie. Everybody starts chanting "Chuy . . . Chuy . . . Chuy!"

Chuy appears onstage with his wife Evelyn and the place goes nuts. Chuy is thanking everybody and suddenly Pickle stands up next to me at our table and says,

"I'm going up there. I started election day with him and I'll end it with him on stage."

And he walks through the crowd in his green sport coat and we watch him. I'm sure Pickle might have later regretted that move, he was all over the papers the next day and on all the TV screens that night. In all the shots of the victory celebration, you can see Chuy and his wife, and just over Chuy's right shoulder, Mike "Pickle" Joyce.

The photo appeared in the Sun-Times the next day and again later on the front page in a slam piece against Pickle . . . but for tonight he was making history in Chicago.

Crawford and I were sitting back watching the whole show, not really interested in jumping up on stage. I'd heard enough stories about the ol' jumping onstage behind the winning candidate routine to try to make that leap. I could just imagine some goo-goo dope stopping me and questioning my commitment to the cause. Would Chuy have vouched for us? Would he even recognize Crawford since they met over a month ago? I remember Peter Nolan writing in his play, THE 51ST WARD, a series of jokes about the ward superintendent Eugene Grigsby who bragged about being one of the "black faces" standing behind Harold Washington the night he was elected and Grigsby's nemesis "Durkin the dirty trickster" says, "There were FIVE THOUSAND black faces on that stage that night!"

But Pickle was all over the TV that night and I got several texts from pals who saw him. He was there all right and it would be only about six weeks before it would come back to bite him in the ass on the front page of the Sun-Times.

So the music started up and the dancing and partying in the

hall started with a bang. I may not have been on the stage but I was interested in stopping by to congratulate my candidate and get a photo together with our crew. So we head up the stairs and the whole joint is mobbed. There's a couple of hard ass bouncers stationed at the door upstairs to Chuy's inner sanctum. It's me, Pickle, and Crawford and we walk up to the door and start to open it when one of these guys stops us.

"Where do you think you're going?"

"We're going in to congratulate Chuy!"

And we pulled the door open. Mister Big Shot tries to stop us but by this time Chuy sees us and runs over and says, "Let these guys in!"

So we're giving out attaboys and shaking his hand and I pull out my camera and hand it to Andrew Sharp, the "campaign manager" and tell him, "Take our picture!"

Sharp acts like I asked him to shine my shoes but tough shit, take the pictures pal.

Chuy has his arms around us and says. "My Los San Patricios!"

It was a cool moment, we felt like we were making history that night in Chicago . . . together.

And we were.

Sharp hands me the camera back and Pickle asks me to take a photo of just him and Chuy.

I posted the photos that night on Facebook with that caption, "Making History in Chicago".

Crawford, Chuy, Houli and Pickle.
Photo courtesy of Mike Houlihan.

Thursday February 26, 2015
Chicagoland

Six shootings last night, including 2 homicides: Albert S. Turner, 23, shot in the chest in Rogers Park, and Demarcus Nelson, 19, shot in the back in Austin.

So it's two days later. We were right where we wanted to be. Crawford and I were in the perfect spot to ask for more dough.

Pickle said, "Get ten grand this time."

And why shouldn't we? That was the deal, get Chuy into a runoff. Maybe we should just keep our mouths shut and hang on for the rest of the ride? On election night I sensed something in the crowd, a movement, the good kind.

We got a shot at this, . . . wouldn't that be sweet. I told Skinny maybe I could be appointed The Commissioner of Tomfoolery.

Maybe, just maybe, Chuy was ready to kick this guy in the ballz.

On election night I watched the tape of Rahm at Plumbers Hall, looking chastened, congratulating Chuy Garcia. He even said something like "Chuy Garcia is a good man." I was astounded, but wary.

He is going to unleash holy hell on all of us.

He spent exactly one day with his new "Mr. Nice Guy" act before his minions worked in the background attempting to destroy the career of one of Chicago's most respected journalists.

On Sunday, Tribune columnist John Kass had written a righteous proposal for the electorate to vote Chuy and put Rahm into a runoff. Kass took sides. And it worked.

The election was Tuesday. On Thursday morning John Kass and his co-host Loren Cohn were summoned into an anteroom at WLS where they were informed that they had both been fired.

Payback? You bet.

Here's my column from freecraic.com

FREE CRAIC Citizens Report American Irish Culture

Amazing Sights in Chicago Mayoral Race, Kass Fired.

Posted on February 28, 2015 by Mike Houlihan

Irish fighters have been celebrated over several centuries because they were seemingly without fear. Some will say that's just because they're hard headed but certainly every tyrant knows that a man with nothing to lose is the most dangerous. Here in Chicago we'll all be able to celebrate that Irish fearlessness in the upcoming mayoral election.

Last Sunday Chicago Tribune columnist John Kass implored the people of Chicago to vote against Mayor Rahm Emanuel and force him into a runoff. On Tuesday, Election Day, that's just what happened. On Wednesday Kass thanked the voters in his column and relished the idea of the coming six-week campaign for Mayor of Chicago.

"In the six weeks to come in this new, extended campaign, Chicago will see some amazing sights.

Like Rahm in the South Side Irish Parade, waving to the crowd and begging for votes, carefully stepping around the clown cars driven by 19th Warders in green hats like the Joyces and the Sheahans."

One of the amazing sights Kass didn't envision was delivered to him the next day. On Thursday Kass was abruptly fired from his job on the radio at WLS, which he'd been doing every morning since 2012.

We can draw our own conclusions of how that came about and WLS had plenty of cover by announcing the return of legendary radio jock Jonathon Brandmeir for Kass's timeslot on their station. Rahm had nothing to do with it. Sure he didn't.

Do you believe that?

Cynics might say it was payback for Kass's attacks on "the nine fingered ballerina", the pejorative nickname given our current Mayor by city workers, cops and firefighters. Cynics might think that Rahm called his brother, the big shot Hollywood agent, and told him, "I need you to deliver a message for me."

Cynics might think the best way to keep the malcontents in line is through fear. Fear for your job, your livelihood, or your family if you dare to question the motives of a Mayor with a Napoleonic complex who rules by fear and fiat.

Irish Americans ruled Chicago for decades. Some of them may have even helped install the current Mayor. But history shows us that the true Irish character in crisis never can be conquered, whether by Cromwell, bloody Maggie, or Paisley. 800 years of oppression forged the Irish character to always stand up to bullies.

So our sympathies to Kass for the guillotine he faced this week. He'll land on his feet and he's still got the Tribune gig. Let's show our solidarity with him and provide some amazing sights of our own.

The best place to start would be the parade.

Saturday, February 28, 2015
Chicagoland

No shootings today!!!

Monday, March 2, 2015
Chicagoland

Seventeen-year-old Deante M. Moard shot in the chest and murdered today in Deering.

Wednesday, March 4, 2015
Chicagoland

Last night there were 8 shootings in Chicago and one homicide, Antonino Walker, 28, shot in the chest in Avalon Park.

Rahm unveils new TV commercial, "Chicago's Future".

When I saw this I couldn't believe it. It opens with a shot of Rahm, wearing a V-neck sweater over a collared shirt eating some humble pie, in what looks like his home. Hey it's Mr. Nice Guy just sitting here to shoot the breeze with us.

He confesses.

"They say your greatest strength can be your greatest weakness. I'm living proof of that. I can rub people the wrong way, or talk when I should listen. I own that."

No shit, Sherlock.

I can't believe that people will be stupid enough to buy this load of horseshit. "I know I'm an asshole, but let me be your asshole."

He's desperate, and it shows. If it weren't for his thirty million bucks in the bank I'd call it today. But never forget the words of Yogi- "it ain't over til it's over."

Friday March 6, 2015
Chicagoland

Six shootings last night, including a 14-year-old male in Grand Boulevard and a 16-year-old male in Grand Crossing.

Okay so now we know the score. Somebody had Kass fired from his radio gig, two days after the election. What a coincidence! Emanuel may or may not have been responsible for that, but my nose smelled a rat and he certainly had a motive. And then groveling in his latest TV spot showed us they were pissed off . . . and scared. And will stop at nothing to destroy us. But I don't really have a job, so Rahm can't get me fired.

Or could he?

That was when I knew I was committed to trying to win this election. I just didn't give a fuck. Rahm's "people" are going to mess with *me*? Bring it on you bastards, and let slip the dogs of war!

We were now getting closer to the high holy days of St. Patrick and the events kicked into high gear.

Friday night, March 6th, was the annual Young Irish Fellowship Paddy's Day party, "Forever Green".

I'd been to the party years back when it was held at Navy Pier. Thousands of young micks slamming beers and puking in their shoes. Ah but I was young then.

Tonight it would be held at Park West in Lincoln Park on Armitage.

This would be a perfect opportunity to show up at the party and meet these young Irish professionals, all of whom vote.

That morning I called Colleen Nolan, the gorgeous redheaded Rose of Tralee, and told her we wanted to bring Chuy to the party.

She was all for it, recognized the excitement it would create in the crowd and said she just had to run it by the board of directors or whoever. Uh oh.

Finally, she calls me back and tells me I have to talk to Conor Kelly and there is a fee.

So I talk to Conor and he tries to talk me out of it with something like $750 in sponsorship fees etc. I'm not crazy about the sound of that, talk him down to $250 and tell him we are coming and let me have our financial guy talk to him.

I call Schaffer and explain that we are being shaken down basically but the cost could well be worth it, if Chuy got to shake a couple thousand hands. Schaffer says "No, it's a great idea and let's spend the money. Have the guy call me and I will give him the credit card number."

Well, that was easy. Too easy.

So I call Conor and let him know we will pay and just call Dave Schaffer at this number and we'll see you tonight. That was my mistake, leaving it in his hands.

I call Crawford and agree to meet him in front of The Billy Goat under the Tribune Tower.

I drive downtown, pick up Billy and we start heading to The Park West. We're psyched, looking forward to a great crowd, lots of young Irish kids, and meeting up with Jack Haines, Red Skelton's illegitimate son, who we met on election night.

So I'm driving up LaSalle Street, about 15 minutes before our scheduled arrival to meet Chuy and his entourage. Crawford is sitting shotgun and I call Clem on the cell.

"Hey Clem, it's Houli."

"Hi."

"Where are you guys?"

"Whaddya mean?"

"We're on our way to the Park West for the Forever Green party, remember we talked earlier today. Chuy is doing a walk thru, huge crowd!"

"Oh yeah, we're not doing that?"

"What?"

"Well we didn't want to do it, sounds like a shakedown, they wanted money."

"Of course they wanted money, Schaffer said he was going to pay."

"Well Chuy's not coming."

"Are you nuts? This is one of the biggest crowds of young voters all in one place, we told them Chuy was coming!"

"Well I'm sorry, but it's not my fault, it's not my fault, it's not my fault!"

What the fuuuuuck! This is a major screw-up.

And I hang up the phone and look at Crawford, "Did you hear that?"

We drove immediately to Lizzie McNeill's Irish pub on the river to commiserate. We are definitely asking for the rest of the dough now. These guys could easily feck up this whole thing, so we better get paid.

It's time to prepare a memo.

March 7, 2015

Chicagoland

Nine shootings, 3 homicides including Jonathon Ramirez 18, Santo Bueno 22, and Juan Marinez 21, stabbed to death.

Minnie Minoso funeral

This morning I call Pickle and relate how Clem and Schaeffer dropped the ball and even Red Skelton's illegitimate son Jack Haines says it was a big mistake for Chuy not to be there.

Pickle says, "Today is Minnie Minoso's funeral, Chuy should be there."

He certainly should be there and I will go with him.

Pickle contacts Clem while I call Christine at the White Sox to arrange a seat for the next mayor of the city of Chicago.

So I get to Holy Family to scope out the situation about an hour before the funeral and chat up Louise, the gal from the White Sox. She's been alerted that Chuy is coming and will have two seats right up front for him. Can I take a look at those seats?

Louise is very gracious and quickly walks up the aisle with me as we shake hands.

"When he arrives come in this side door and I will walk him to his seat."

Cool.

So I'm standing in front of Holy Family wearing a suit and tie on this Saturday morning and watching Chicago's hall of famers pay their final respects to Orestes Minoso. ***Orestes "Minnie" Miñoso*** The first Black Cuban in the major leagues and the first black player in White Sox history, as a 1951 rookie he was one of the first Latin Americans to play in a MLB All-Star Game. Minoso was the only man in professional baseball history to play in six decades.

I'm getting cell phone calls from Chuy's guys, how far away he is. They are ready to close the doors to the church and start the funeral. I'd been standing in front of church for at least a half hour shooting the breeze with Judge Mark Ballard, who lives nearby and is walking his dog, (Muggsy, a Boston Terrier that, for some reason, chicks love).

Muggsy the dog. Photo courtesy of Mark Ballard.

We're talking politics as attractive women keep coming up to pet his dog and he says, "You think Chuy can win, Houli?"

"Yeah I do, the emperor has no clothes, the city is totally fecked."

Mark is wisely noncommittal, wearing a jacket that says, "The White House" monogramed on the breast, and it appears legit. He's a sitting Cook County judge, no reason to think he's never been to The White House.

So we're standing there while I wait for Chuy and hope they don't screw up another one. The church is packed with media and it will definitely get covered on all the TV news broadcasts. Free media!

Former Fire Commissioner Jimmy Joyce and retired copper Billy Nelligan walk up to the church and say hi. They're city of Chicago legends but they came today as White Sox fans.

I introduce the lads to Judge Ballard and Joyce says to Mark, "Hey weren't you in the White House?"

Love watching old school Southsiders bust balls!

Finally, the casket is being wheeled off the hearse and up the front stairs of the church. Minnie is about to take his final trot around the bases.

Where the fuck is Chuy?

The undertaker closes the door of the church and I'm standing at the bottom of the stairs, and my heart is pounding, and suddenly they show up in a black SUV.

I open the door for Chuy and tell him, "You just made it, come on."

We hustle in the side door and I catch Louise's attention, she comes right up to us and I introduce her to Chuy.

"Good morning Commissioner, I have two seats for you, please just follow me."

There's another guy with Chuy, Paul Brozek from Bridgeport. Nice guy, I have no idea if he is sitting with Chuy or not. So there's three of us headed to the pew and I know only two seats. She takes us to the first pew in the section right behind the family. To our right sit Mayor Rahm Emmanuel, and former Mayor Richard M. Daley and his brother Cook County Commissioner John Daley. Sitting in the pew beside us is White Sox Hall of Famer, The Big Hurt, Frank Thomas.

As Chuy enters the pew, I genuflect and tell Paul, "I'll take it from here."

The mass begins.

So I'm scanning the crowd for characters and can feel the bad vibes being emanated from Rahm in his pew. Media is filming the whole thing, and it's televised LIVE.

Chicago White Sox great, the late Billy Pierce, got up and gives a great eulogy for his old pal.

"Minnie Minoso never said a bad word about anybody."

And I believed him.

And felt suddenly humbled. Man, I felt ashamed. I've bad mouthed plenty of good people, in case you haven't been reading this book up til now. But If I was *that* nice a guy, this would be a different story.

Sure we were all nice people, trying to do the city some good. Sure . . . but that's not what actually happened.

Minnie's son then gets up and talks about his dad. And he starts bawling like crazy, and this guy is no kid. And he's crying, "Daddy... daddy, we love you so."

I wanted to grab him by the shoulders and tell him, "Snap out of it, in case you didn't know it, your old man was about a hundred and six feckin' years old, for cripesakes! He had a helluva run!"

And then the words of Billy Pierce echoed in my ears, "Minnie Minoso never said a bad word about anybody."

Shame on me.

I didn't know until I got in the car on the way home, but me and Chuy were all over the TV during the funeral broadcast. Mike Flood texted me a screen grab from his TV of me and Chuy in the pew and I looked exactly like my dad. I had no idea I looked that feckin' old!

Screen grab Courtesy: CSN Chicago

As the funeral ended, and the pews leave in order starting at the front, the Daley brothers, Rich and John, made their way across the aisle to say hello to Chuy and wished him well. They shook my hand too, and smiled as if to say, "I have no idea who the fuck you are." Across the aisle I felt ice pick daggers shooting from the corner of Rahm's eyes as he walked out in front of us.

We walked down the aisle and many Sox fans reached out to shake Chuy's hand. He was diggin' it.

"Good job Houli, how did you set this up?"

I called the White Sox.

The crowd was backed up on the stairs while the pall bearers loaded Minnie back into the hearse and I turned and said to Frank "The Big Hurt" Thomas, "So how are things in Berwyn?"

Frank had opened a restaurant in my hood at Cermak and Oak Park Ave. and it looked like they were doing pretty good business. "Berwyn is going good."

I told him I was the Baron of Berwyn. I don't think he got it.

Monday, March 9, 2015

Chicagoland

Nine shootings last night, including the gunshot murders of Linda Soto 25, as well as the arson death of Mary A. Noble, 79.

To: Clem Balanoff, Chuy Garcia for Mayor Campaign, Dave Schaeffer, Mike Joyce,

From: Mike Houlihan, Bill Crawford

This is a crucial week for the campaign with the two parades and a variety of Irish related events leading up to the parades. You guys hired us to get Chuy into this community and here's our strategy for the week.

Please don't be "penny-wise and pound-foolish" as you were last week with Friday's "Forever Green 40" Party at Park West. Because you didn't want to spend $250 for a political sponsorship package, you missed an opportunity to meet over 1,000 young voters that night and the reception would have been significant. Please don't blow any more opportunities like this. If we recommend an event or a marketing opportunity, it's because we know this audience and we are confident that the time and money are well spent.

This is the biggest week of the year in the biggest month of the year for the Irish American electorate. They love politics and they all vote, so let's get Chuy out there to ask for their votes.

Friday March 13, 8AM, Union League Club.

Irish American Partnership breakfast. All the big hitters will be there, Alderman Ed Burke usually chairs the event, great opportunity to upstage Rahm. It's $175 per person, but well worth it. Let me know and I will get Chuy a good seat and he will get to meet everybody, the best part is the schmooze starting around 7:15AM.

Friday March 13. Noon to 3PM Blue Cross Blue Shield Labor Affairs St. Patrick's Party

Plumbers Hall 1340 W. Washington

Chuy would be my guest. This is almost exclusively labor leaders and political insiders, a great opportunity to meet and greet. Peak time is around 1PM.

Friday March 13, 6PM. Hilton Towers Hotel. 114th Annual Irish Fellowship Club St. Pat's Dinner

This is the big dog, probably close to a thousand voters at this. Gotta do this. $175 per head, we will find you a good table.

Saturday, March 14, Chicago's 60th Annual St. Patrick's Day Parade, steps off at noon from Balbo and Columbus.

We should have Chuy march in the front line with all the other politicians, Rahm etc, and then double back to march with the Teamsters or Teachers Union contingents. This is televised by WLS. Need marchers with Chuy signs for the double back.

Post Parade Party for Mercy Home, checking this out for more info.

Sunday March 15, 2015 Southside Irish Parade

Kicks off from 103rd and Western at noon. There is a Mass in the morning at St. Cajetan's, this would be a great spot for Chuy to attend Sunday mass before the parade, and it will be packed. Mike Joyce has a group, The Celtic Boxing Club, which Chuy will march with. Lots of kids wearing Chuy t-shirts etc. Then post parade parties in the Beverly neighborhood to meet and greet voters.

You didn't want to spend the money for a full page ad in February or March issues of the Irish American News, but I can still get you in the April issue that comes out on April 1st. The deadline for this, with money up front, is March 15th. I'm going to write my "Hooliganism" column on Chuy and endorse him in this issue. Take the ad, it's cheap and the Irish will see it and vote for Chuy.

Our initial proposal covered the campaign up to the runoff and obviously we are still working on the campaign. **At this point though, we need another check for $5,000 so let me know when I can pick it up.**

Thanks,

Houli and Bill

Yeah, I know I snuck it in there at the end, but I don't think those mopes ever read that far down to see it.

I figured if we were ever gonna get any *more* money from the campaign, this weekend would be the one to squeeze them.

From now through St. Patrick's Day the Irish do a very good job of trying to remind everybody, we're still in charge!

If you are running for mayor of the city of Chicago you had better have some very good, kiss-kiss, lip service for the Irish American community. At least for this weekend! It's our turn for cryin' out loud.

We want reparations for the 800 years of oppression we suffered at the hands of the Brits!

Wednesday March 11, 2015
Chicagoland

Four shootings today across the city.

The Skinny & Houli Show.

Skinny and I record the show tonight at Lizzie McNeill's Irish Pub with Irish fiddler Katie Grennan, and the visiting delegation from County Cork Ireland, including their Mayor, as guests on our show. The Irish spirit has kicked in completely in Chicago now and we're having a blast.

After the show Skinny and I are talking about the campaign. He is a volunteer with Special Olympics, helping them organize events and raising money for them. He has to be very careful regarding the mayoral campaign, particularly because Rahm Emanuel has helped him in the past with the Polar Plunge, etc. So he won't attack Rahm, as I have been doing for weeks. But I've never used our show as a forum for talking about what an asshole the mayor is, in deference to my co-host and our sponsors. But I've been very vocal in my monthly column in the Irish American News and on Facebook.

So Skinny and I are shooting the breeze after the show over several beers and he's asking me about the campaign. I give voice to my frustrations with the "progressives" running the campaign and how they can't seem to pull the trigger on a full on assault on the mayor, something I would like to see happen. Sometimes I have the subtlety of a sledge hammer.

Rahm has thirty million bucks to make Chuy look like a dumb Mexican and we can't seem to get any traction on our attacks. After my sixth Guinness I say to Skinny, "Geez, it's just a matter of time before Rahm plays his "Jewish" card.

"What?"

"Sure, you know eventually they will be accusing Chuy of being anti-Semitic. That's gotta be in their playbook for sure. It's Saul Alinsky 101. It's how he beat Nancy Kaszak for Congress, accused her of being endorsed by a Jew hater."

"What if you beat them to it? Call a press conference and have Chuy say, "'I am not anti-Semitic."'

The midnight logic of this is astounding to me and I counter to Skinny. "Not only that, but I am not a racist or misogynist either. Nor am I homophobic or Islamaphobic! We could take all their cards away with one press conference!"

I filed this stroke of genius away when my phone rang, it was Pickle.

Supposedly Pickle has a line on a group of wealthy donors who were about to make a big drop on Chuy's campaign, now that he is in the runoff. I ask Pickle about the timing of this donation because Crawford and I are about to put the touch on the campaign for another five grand. Have those fat cat donors delivered their check yet?

Pickle tells me, "the money has already been wired directly into the campaign account!"

I decide then and there that tomorrow Crawford and I are going down to campaign headquarters and pick up our check for five large.

Now you'd think that Rahm would have the Jewish vote locked up, but there was still some lingering resentment about Rahm's connection to Obama when he was Chief of Staff. Obama wasn't exactly chummy with Bibi Netanyahu and on top of that. many of the Jewish old timers aren't fans of Rahm's style, particularly his vulgar language and obnoxious behavior. They were repulsed by Rahm, his despicable behavior calling people 'retards', telling women 'F-you', shouting at people to 'take your tampons out', sending dead fish to enemies, humping chairs in Grant park, confronting people while nude in the locker room, all the Rahm 'shtick'.

They have an old Yiddish expression, Shanda fur di Goyim!-be careful of your behavior in gentile company.

When I get home I tell my wife, "We're gonna have Chuy call a press conference where he announces that he is NOT anti-Semitic."

She says, "Are you out of your mind? How many beers did you have tonight?"

Thursday March 12, 2015
Chicagoland

3 shootings today in Woodlawn, Lower West Side, and Grand Crossing.

I pick up Crawford today and we head down to the campaign office to pick up our check. On the phone with Pickle he informs me that one of his guys, Steve Collier, is now working security for the campaign. Steve is a very large black man, has to be almost seven feet tall, played with several teams in the NFL, including the Packers, as a defensive end and offensive tackle. He's a giant.

Steve Collier with Houli. Photo courtesy of Mike Joyce.

We can't find a parking space so Crawford waits in the car in front, "This shouldn't take long, I will be right out."

Marty O'Connor's mantra, "get the money, everything else is

nonsense" plays in my head as I walk in the door, and a shadow falls across my entrance, blocking out the sun. I look up into the eyes of one of the largest human being I have ever seen.

"Hey, you must be Steve."

"Uh yeah, how can I help you."

"I'm Houli, Pickle's pal".

"Oh yeah, Pickle."

"Welcome to the campaign."

"Thanks, what you need?"

"I'm here to see Clem."

And I start to walk past him, but Steve stops me.

"Wait a minute Houli, I have to make sure he's here."

This guy is really scary but I don't give a shit and I start scanning the room for Clem.

"Hey Clem, Clem . . . I'm here to pick up our check!"

Steve affectionately puts his arm on my shoulder, "Hold on a second Houli, we'll find him."

My blood pressure is rising and I now have the attention of the entire office.

Clem comes out of his office, followed by press secretary Monica Trevino, an angel.

"Hey Clem, I got Crawford waitin' out in the car, we gotta big week coming up, so I wanna pick up our check."

"What check?"

I can feel the eyes of all of these progressive dildos in the campaign office looking at me as they watch the scene unfold and that old snark starts to climb up my back.

"The check for the five grand, for our services, that was the deal, get Chuy in the runoff, and we get paid again. It's all in the memo I sent ya."

"What memo?"

"Hey . . . what the feck Clem, don't make me have to ask my guy Steve here, to turn you upside down".

And I pointed to Steve standing behind me, jokingly of course.

"Your guy, ah no he's my guy."

"Hey let's stop with the bullshit Clem, I want the five grand . . . now."

Suddenly Monica Trevino intervenes, "Mike, please, come on back to the office and let's talk this through, obviously there has been a misunderstanding."

"Just write me a check, you can make it out to Crawford, he's waiting in the car. Five grand."

Clem looks crazed, "Five grand? We don't have five grand! We're practically broke and we need money for more TV."

I smile at Monica and tell Clem, with a very smug look on my face— "Come on Clem, I know you guys have the money, Pickle told me his big shot donors wired the dough directly into the campaign account."

Everything stopped in the room.

I could feel a pin drop . . . on to my testicles.

Clem gets this demented look on his face, like somebody had just told him the most hilarious joke. "Oh so..Pickle told you that, huh?"

I can feel the first bead of sweat breaking out on my upper lip. I feel the hand of Steve Collier on my shoulder and he says, "Why don't I call Pickle right now? We can ask him."

Ssssure.

The jig is up, and it's my turn in the barrel.

I turn and look at the room full of goo-goo's watching me squirm and they are loving it, but they're still a bit scared that something or *someone* might go haywire.

Steve hands me the phone.

"Pickle? Hi . . . Mike . . . lemme tell you where I am right now, I'm standing in the foy-A of the campaign office, I'm with Clem, and Monica, and Steve. And I just told them about the money being wired directly into the account, . . . so . . . so I guess that was bullshit, right?"

I can hear Pickle screaming into the phone, "What difference does it make?" He sounded like Hillary Clinton . . . y'know . . . guilty.

I hand the phone back to Steve the giant. He looks like he feels sorry for me. He could have easily pummeled me for my behavior, but he was compassionate.

I was humiliated and pissed off and embarrassed.

"Well I'm gonna leave now, sorry about that. Yeah that Pickle is . . . quite a card. Clem take a look at the memo, it outlines our services for the rest of the campaign, and get me the money when you can.

Sorry to have bothered you."

I storm out the door and back to the car, Crawford is sitting in the front seat, sleeping.

He peeks from under his hat, with a quizzled look about him. "How did it go? Didja get the check?"

"Fuck no I didn't

gleta/kn&$*nfg#;fk@!dnea'knflvkmelmffkm!!!!!"

I was frothing at the mouth.

"That fucking Pickle is full of shit!"

I start telling him the story and suddenly there is a knock on the passenger side door, it's Steve Collier.

Crawford looks up at him and then at me with horror on his face. This is it, curtains for Crawford!

I roll the window down and he says, "Hey Houli, Pickle wants you to call him. You dropped your hat too."

He hands me my hat that had somehow fallen off in my fury.

"Thanks Steve, watch out for that guy Pickle, he just fucked us royally with his stupid bullshit."

"I hear ya, Houli."

Friday, March 13, 2015

Chicagoland

Seven shootings today, including an 18-year-old male in Lawndale who shot himself in his junk.

Blue Cross/Blue Shield Paddy's Day Party

Dick Quigley is the labor guy for Blue Cross/Blue Shield and they are the insurance providers for many of Chicago's very healthy unions. They host two parties a year, celebrating Christmas and St. Patrick's

Day. I've been going to the parties for years, thanks to the hospitality of Frank Harmon and now Dick Quigley.

Lots of big shots are at the party; pols, union guys, and those who want union business. The Queen of the Parade and her court make an appearance and it's not unusual to see somebody campaigning in the crowd.

The party was held in the basement of Plumber's Hall with its oval mahogany bar about fifty yards around. They had union bartenders too, the best!

Chuy had lots of union support, but not with Local 399, Local 150, or Local 130 that's for sure. So it was going to be a mixed crowd at best, but the corned beef and cabbage dinner was a bloodbath compared to this.

Things were different now. Chuy now had a legitimate shot and was deemed worthy of some respect. Just in case he wasn't, I called Dick Quigley and let him know I intended on bringing our candidate to the party as my guest.

Quigley was thrilled! "It will bring some excitement to the party."

Chuy showed up accompanied by Alderman Ricardo Munoz, so it was two of the top dog Latinos working the Paddy's Day Party at Plumbers Hall. As I escorted my amigos into the bar I told Chuy, "This is called bearding the lion in his den."

We get a great reception from all assembled and the plumbers can't say shit cuz this is not their party. I bump into Skinny with our old pal Ronnie Morasso as we make our way through the room and take him aside.

"Hey Skin, I'm thinkin' maybe that "Jewish Card" thing, y'know about Chuy holding the press conference? We talked about it last night, ain't such a good idea. Maybe we didn't really think that through?"

We both start laughing and chalk it up to scheming while skating. Let's stay positive.

The rest of the afternoon is great with all labor guys loving Chuy.

**Friday March 13, 2015 Irish Fellowship Club of Chicago St.
Patrick's Day Dinner, Hilton Towers.**

After Plumber's Hall I had just enough time to swing by my office,
grab a nap, and then head to the Hilton for the big soiree of the season.
I'd received a phone call from Schaffer a day or two earlier and he tells
me he has arranged for Chuy to be feted at the Wabash Tap, owned by
the O'Malley brothers, right before the parade steps off on Saturday.
Schaffer puts Mark O'Malley on the phone to schmooze me and he
says he will have about 200 supporters in the bar to greet Chuy before
the parade, bring him there around 10:45AM. I call Pickle about this
and he says, "Schaffer should be careful about those O'Malley's."

The O'Malley's also owned The Firehouse on Michigan Ave and
had been long time friends and supporters of Mayor Richard M.
Daley. They also owned the Park Grille in Millennium Park and had
supposedly gotten a sweetheart deal on garbage, water, and taxes from
the city, thanks to Rich.

They'd gotten some bad press because of that, and Rahm was suing
the O'Malley Brothers, hence Pickle telling me Schaffer should be
careful.

I forget about it and head over to the Hilton wearing my "Chuy"
button.

At the bar in Kitty O'Shea's I wait with a couple of Pickle's cousins.

Sitting across from us in the bar is Local 150 big heat Jimmy
McNally. He's waiting for his family and does <u>not</u> bust my balls over
the Chuy button. Local 150 is also a sponsor of my radio show so I'm
not really looking to piss him off. He's great as usual and we toast to
St. Patrick.

Vince Winters comes by from Local 399 and wants to know why
I'm with Chuy. "He's paying me". That's good enough for him, and
when I ask why he is with Rahm he says, "Look at all the cranes all
over the city, it's the work."

Get the money, everything else is nonsense.

I call our candidate to find out his ETA and Rick Munoz answers
the phone, "Where are you guys?"

He asks me, "Is Schaffer with you?"

"No, but I'm sitting with our hosts the Harvey's and if you guys don't' get here soon, the crowd will have gone into the dining room.

So hurry up and meet us in Kitty O'Shea's."

Five minutes later Chuy and Munoz walk in the door. We immediately start guiding him through the bar to shake hands and the reaction is glee from the characters assembled.

"Let's get upstairs now and work the big cocktail hour crowd."

The place is packed and the Irish are out in force for the big night. I'm getting the fish eye from some, but most are happy to meet "the next mayor of the city of Chicago".

We come across Cyril Regan, the man from Roscommon, who I've heard so much about and he joins the entourage. Chuy says, "I can't believe you guys don't know each other!"

I know him now and he was a great asset for the campaign and connections to the Irish community over the next few final weeks.

As we weave our way through the crowd with Chuy shaking hands, there are conflicting receptions and we almost bump into Rahm right there. Local 399 is giving us the stink eye as Brian Hickey is arguing with one of Pickle's cousins, who happens to also be a cousin of Brian's! Southside shit.

Everybody wants selfies with Chuy and he tells me he has to go to another fundraiser immediately and won't be staying for dinner, that's good, maybe I might get to do some actual drinkin' at this event.

Chuy exits and we breathe a sigh of relief that he was able to make an appearance and create a buzz in the night. One of the cousins is talking my ear off in the lobby about the nine-fingered- ballerina and I see him standing about ten feet away. I tell her, "Do you know who is standing right behind you?"

She says, "I know, the devil!"

I sit down to dinner and drinks with whoever I was freeloading from that night. On the way to the pisser I run into Mark O'Malley and his wife in the lobby. "See you tomorrow!"

Saturday March 14, 2015

Chicagoland

Five shootings today and one man found dead in Englewood.

Chicago's St. Patrick's Day Parade

This is it, the apex of our campaign for the Irish white ethnic vote. I got up early to preview the day. I was meeting Chuy and Schaffer et al at The Wabash Tap, a pub in the South Loop owned by the O'Malley Brothers. Schaffer had called me on the phone yesterday to put Mark O'Malley on the line and explain that they were hosting a morning breakfast for Chuy before the parade, a pre-parade meet and greet.

So we're scheduled to meet up at the Wabash Tap around 10:45. Parade steps off at noon, so time was gonna be tight. I was anxious about the parade because I knew it would mean a confrontation with the Plumbers, as they controlled who would march in the front line. Rahm of course, along with Preckwinkle and other elected Dems. But Chuy was a Cook County Commissioner, so "you have to let him in the parade!"

Regardless, I knew they were gonna beef.

On top of that I'm still a bit hungover from the Guinness last night and as I get on the Ike headed east to the Loop, I start thinking that the old Guinness scutter might be kicking in.

The "scutter" is that old irregular gurgling that usually signals a prelude to explosions in my gut. The Irish call it the Guinness scutter. If you're not familiar with the "scutter", it means spending lots of quality time on the toilet in the morning. This could potentially throw a wrench into my marching plan that day. But I decided to just place that in the good Lord's hands and play the cards I am dealt.

I'm silently saying the rosary in the car on the way down and my phone blows up. It's Pickle.

"Where are you going?"

"I'm going down to the Wabash Tap to meet Chuy before the parade."

"NO, that's not going to happen."

"It's not?"

"That would be a mistake for Chuy to be seen with the O'Malley's. They are being sued by Rahm."

When their scandal broke in The Sun-Times for the "sweetheart" deal they cut to get the restaurant in Millennium Park, they used the same photo of the brothers, Mark and Matt, that had once graced a column I wrote in the Sun-Times about them opening a new restaurant, Grainne O'Malley's.

So I remembered telling them, one afternoon at Gene and Georgetti's, when the photo was splashed all over the Sun-Times that I hope you don't think I had anything do with that! Cuz it was the same photo from my column, see.

But I also remembered, when interviewing the lads for the column about their new restaurant, that my kid was looking for a bartending job and asking maybe they could help him out?

And they did, they hired him . . . For one day.

And then cut him loose.

I remembered that too.

So I think maybe Pickle is over-reacting and tell him so. But he hangs up and the next thing I know, Clem is on the line telling me to "abort" and just meet Chuy and the rest of them directly across the street from where the parade kicks off-in the lobby of the Hilton.

I can do that, as I remembered that the Hilton has a great mens crapper. I would have just enough time to attend to the "scutter" in one of the nicest rest rooms in town. Sometimes they even had a guy there to turn on the water for you.

The Hilton Lobby on parade weekend is nuts with Irish, huge line out to the street trying to get into Kitty O'Shea's, lots of private party brunches before the parade. The staging area for the parade is only about a football field away from the entrance of the Hilton. The lobby actually is very elegant and it's just buzzing with folks who had booked rooms after the Irish Fellowship dinner, and were now going to hit the parade.

So fast forward to me in the lobby of the Hilton after parking the car on Wabash. I've got a good half hour before I have to meet Chuy at 11:30 and I'm looking forward to a nice leisurely dump.

I'm sitting on the throne contemplating the campaign and my phone starts blowing up. My coat is hanging on the hook on the back of the stall door and I lean forward and reach into the pocket to retrieve it.

Thank God I had entered O'Malley's phone number into the phone yesterday when Schaffer had called from his phone. So my caller ID is blinking,

"Mark O'Malley"

While the phone makes it obnoxious jingle and I'm sitting and thinking, well I don't think I wanna take this call. He's probably in his tavern with a couple hundred "Chuy supporters" he's recruited, wondering where the hell we are?

"Mark O'Malley"

Finally, he gives up, leaves a voice mail and I put the phone back in the coat pocket.

A couple of seconds, and it starts ringing again.

"Mark O'Malley!!!"

No I don't think so, Mark.

"Mark O'Malley!!!!"

Oh for fuck sakes. Leave a message I'm taking a crap for cryin' out loud!

I start laughing to myself as I remembered how they helped my kid with that bartender job, for one day. We hadn't called them to ask what happened, we just figured out that there had never really been a job for my kid. Well today maybe O'Malley would figure out that Chuy wasn't coming to their party.

I chuckled to myself at the the irony of it all.

Yeah, they'll figure it out.

After tidying up at the marble sinks in the Hilton crapper, I made my way out to the lobby, still had about ten minutes before the scheduled arrival of Chuy.

I'm exiting the men's room and I bump into my old pal Marty Mullarkey. Marty is the concierge for McCormick Place and has been called, among other things, the unofficial mayor of McCormick Place. He's about 6'5', just a biscuit under 350lbs with an engaging wit and gregarious personality. He loves politicians, to him they are the movie stars of Chicago, and will stop at nothing to rub shoulders with a variety of Democratic fakers.

Chicago's St. Patrick's Day parade is probably the biggest day of the year for Marty. He will find a way to march as close to the front line as he can get, then he will double back to march with other groups like the Shannon Rovers, or a local Ward organization, as he handshakes his way across the city.

Back when I was writing for the Sun-Times, I interviewed Marty for my "Houli in 'da Hood" column and you'd think I had loaned him money the way he ate it up. He carried the clipping with him for months afterward.

When Sis Daley died, she was waked at Nativity parish in Bridgeport. Marty was first in line to inform Mayor Rich Daley of his condolences. Later in the back of the church, Marty showed off his clippings to the assembled ward healers.

Skinny Sheahan supposedly remarked to Daley, "Didja see Marty Mullarkey?", to which Daley retorted, "Did I see him? He practically held his own press conference at my mother's wake!"

So Marty gives me the big hello in the lobby of the Hilton and he's dressed in his standard black suit with green carnation and his slicked-back, black Irish hair. "Who 'ya marchin' with, Houli?"

I show him my Chuy button, and bust his balls, "I'm marching with the next mayor of the city of Chicago, Jesus "Chuy" Garcia!"

Seated in the lobby, and within earshot is lobbyist Bill Gainer. Gainer is solidly with the Rahminator and he is not too pleased to see my Chuy button. He castigates me for wearing it, as if I had somehow broken some phony Southside Irish pledge to vote for the incumbent. "What the hell do you think you're doing?"

I scoff at him and make a mental note of his umbrage. I didn't know I needed his permission to support whoever I wish. It's a free feckin' country, last I heard.

Irked, I head over to the main lobby where I am scheduled to meet the entourage.

Chuy arrives with Rick Munoz and a few followers, including Cyril Regan, the man from County Roscommon, Ireland. Cyril runs several businesses in the Chicagoland area and loves politics. He is a devotee of Cook County Board President Toni Preckwinkle, who put him on to Chuy and we've become great pals.

Cyril is wearing the black suit and shades that is the uniform of most Secret Service. He looks the part and it helps as he guides Chuy through the crowd.

We walk up to the parade staging area and I know it's going to get ugly now. I had called Mike Tierney from Local 130 a few nights back to make sure we would have a spot in the lineup. He was not happy. "You have no idea what the fuck you are doing."

Okay, just give me the dope and save the lecture pal. Funny how everybody gets bent out of shape when you don't fall in line. I've never been a follower, especially of little shits who come from the North Shore and work for the Clintons and Obamas and expect me to kiss their ass and surrender the city I grew up in. Not me. Happy to take your dough Plumbers, but you don't own me.

We cross the bridge on Balbo and make our way to the staging area. It's a gorgeous day for a parade, sun is out and the crowd is thick. They are all there, 99.99% Democrats; Madigan, Daley, Rahm, Preckwinkle, and their assorted ass kissers; jockeying for position. I see Mike Tierney out of the corner of my eye as we bring Chuy to the fore.

The media immediately senses Chuy's presence and descend on us, surrounding him and peppering him with questions. Tierney grabs me and pulls me aside. "You're NOT in the front line!"

Fine, where should we line up?

"In back, back there" ... he points south and I see Jesse White wearing his sash and schmoozing folks. "Back with Jesse White!"

Ain't nothing wrong with that. I corral Chuy and our gang and we line up around Secretary of State Jesse White. He welcomes us warmly; he's got no dog in this fight.

It's funny to watch all these lace curtain flannel mouth phonies running around with top hats on and sashes and carnations acting like they rule the world. The bagpipes are bleating and the drums are pounding and everybody looks happy, except Mike Tierney.

We're waiting to start marching and I see Toni Preckwinkle walk back to us to shake Chuy's hand. Oh thanks for acknowledging us. She's the one who wanted to run for mayor but didn't have the cojones to challenge Rahm. She's the President of the Cook County Board and Jesus Chuy Garcia is her floor leader, but she was too scared of Rahm to endorse Chuy, knowing she would pay for it later if Rahm won. Toni you are true Chicago profile in courage.

Thanks for nothin'.

The whistles blow and 1953 Heisman Trophy winner, the late Johnny Lattner, carrying the banner of St. Patrick, leads us off up Columbus Drive with the Shannon Rovers as the 2015 Chicago St. Patrick's Day parade steps off.

As we descend into the morass of Columbus Blvd, it becomes clear that the crowd loves Chuy. You can hear them shouting "Chew-ey, Chew-ey, Chew-ey!" as we move down the parade route. Chuy wisely breaks from the group to engage the folks along the route on the sidelines, shaking hands, high fiving, and laughing as he goes. He's a natural and the crowd is screaming for him as he zig zags across the parade route sharing the love.

Clem Balanoff is running around like a chicken with his head cut off and Cyril is doing his best Secret Service impression. I'm jogging along and hoping not to break a sweat. But it's all good.

Midway through the parade, right around Buckingham Fountain, I spy my old pal Bob Ryan on the reviewing stand. Bob and I did the plumbing commercials together for years and I stupidly assume he will plug Chuy on the PA system. I run over with Chuy and wave to Bob and I see a look of pure terror in his eyes.

Bob is not going to say shit of course, because this is Local 130's show and if he gives Chuy a plug it might be the end of his pension with the plumbers. I'm shouting, "Bob, Bob, we got Chuy here." But

Bob is not taking the bait, can't say as I blame him. All I can get out of him is "Happy St. Patrick's Day everybody."

The marshals appear and tell us to keep it moving. Of course we gotta keep it moving or we could get hit in the head by a flying Jesse White Tumbler as we march down the parade route.

We see Frank Mathie from ABC News doing sideline bits and he does a quickie with Chuy, God bless him and the crowd is just going nuts, "Chew-eey, Chew-eey, Chew-eey!"

It's all a blur after that until we reach the end of the parade, north of Monroe Street. Eddie Burke is there to greet us, at least he welcomes Chuy, "Happy St. Patrick's Day Mr. Commissioner". The Consul General of Ireland is there as well and I'm scanning the crowd for Rahm.

Chuy breaks for the horse shoe of parade goers at the end of the street and is shaking hands and getting patted on the back and suddenly I see Rahm come out of the crowd that looked like it swallowed him up. He erupts from the crowd, lost in the people without his handlers, looking pissed. He's got a stressed look on his face and who knows what some of those micks just said to him, in the scrum, but he's not happy. Looks like his security detail got lost and he and Chuy almost bump right into each other as the Rahmster makes his way back to a safer spot.

I try to set up a photo with Chuy and Eddie Burke and Irish Consul General Aidan Cronin, but Cronin is having none of it. No way he wants his photo in the paper with Chuy. Amazing the fear this little nine- fingered-ballerina strikes in the hearts of men. I remark to Cyril Regan about Cronin taking a duck and he says, "Feck him, he's a civil servant!"

Well this guy's got moxie I figure and we head back to the hotel.

Mission accomplished.

*   *   *

Sunday, March 15, 2015. The Ides of March

Chicagoland

Fifteen shootings today, four murders including gunshot victims Andre Chatman 23, Larry Hollis 28, Giovani Matos 16, and 19-year-old Talal Aljohan was stabbed to death in Albany Park.

Southside Irish St. Patrick's Day Parade

"Chuy" Garcia to march with Celtic Boxing Club in South Side Irish Parade on Sunday

St. Rita High School alum and Chicago Mayoral contender Jesus "Chuy" Garcia will march with young members of the Celtic Boxing Club at the South Side Irish St. Patrick's Day Parade this Sunday, March 15th.

Garcia joins other prominent members of The Celtic Boxing Club for the parade, including former South Side Irish Parade Grand Marshall and boxing champion "Irish" John Collins, United States Olympic boxer and World Champion David Diaz, and Rasheda and Jamillah Ali, the twin daughters of the legendary Muhammad Ali.

The Celtic Boxing Club is a youth sports program located in Chicago's Mt. Greenwood/Beverly neighborhood. Over the years the Celtic Boxing Club has used the sport of boxing to teach young people the values of hard work, discipline, respect for others and a sense of community. Since 1977 The Celtic Boxing Club has performed boxing exhibitions to raise hundreds of thousands of dollars for worthy charities and causes. For more information please visit http://celticboxing.com

We met at Pickle's house before the parade. Early that morning Pickle got a call from John Kass's legman asking if Rahm was

marching in the South Side Parade, because it had just been pulled
from the Mayor's schedule for the day. Word on the street was that
Rahm would now be marching with the unions because he feared
getting booed if he marched alone as Mayor of the City of Chicago.
Of course he still got booed, hey it's the southside.

Knowing my pals on the south side, they would indeed have booed,
and razzed, and chastised Rahm for being a little weasely pimp. But
the sanctuary of the unions kept a barrier there that would protect
the Mayor.

I went to early Mass that morning at St. Odilo's parish in Berwyn.
I knew this was going to be a long day and I wanted to be fortified. I
arrived at Pickle's house around 11AM. Crawford would be meeting
me there along with Cyril Regan. In typical fashion Pickle is not ready
and leaves me to babysit his 4-year-old kid in the kitchen while he
grabs a shower. His wife Jamillah, daughter of Muhammed Ali, is
already over at the float with her twin sister Rasheda.

So I'm sitting on the floor with Jake, the grandson of Muhammed
Ali, as we play Legos on the floor and talk about the election.

The Southside Irish St. Patrick's Day parade was founded in . . . well
to enlighten you about the parade, let me reprint here an article I
wrote in The Irish American News back in 2012:

March 2012

Irish American News

The Legend of Skinny Sheahan

It might be the greatest hoax in Chicago political history.

*Percolating in the brainpan of Skinny Sheahan ever since his
beloved Southside Irish Parade was canceled by a wussy wing of
the parade committee three years ago. Ruffians had "hi-jacked"
the parade and instead of cracking down, the committee decided
to capitulate, castrate it, and then cry about it.*

It left the community without the touchstone they'd taken for granted for the last 32 years.

I delivered a eulogy at a "wake" for the parade at The Beverly Woods banquet hall at 115ᵗʰ and Western on the day the parade should have been in 2010. Skinny stood in the back with Irish TD Jimmy Deenihan and predicted to Sun-Times reporter Mark Konkol, "The parade will be back."

He said it very matter of factly, as though he knew something nobody else had considered. It was a gauntlet tossed in the face of all those opposed to the parade and over the course of the next two years it would become just what he had stated, a fact.

Last August the movement to resurrect the parade began in earnest at a public meeting at The Beverly Art Center where everyone was invited to discuss the reasons the parade was canceled and if there was any interest in bringing it back. As I walked into the meeting there was Mark Konkol of the Sun-Times once again chronicling our world.

At this meeting we heard all the familiar complaints of public intoxication, urination, defecation, and even fornication on neighbor's lawns during the parade. All agreed this was a bad thing and all agreed we could do better. Skinny Sheahan stood on the stage and guided the conversation, encouraging folks to vent or lament the loss of the parade.

He asked for a show of hands against the resurrection of the parade. I saw only one man, a transplant to the neighborhood, raise his hand. A plan was taking shape in the mind of Skinny.

Meetings continued throughout the next six months and the business community stepped up with pledges of over $90,000 to *defray the extra costs of security and to bolster the $100,000 that had been raised annually by the committee. On the radio and in person Skinny evangelized for a "zero tolerance" parade that would return to the traditions of family and faith embraced by all the Irish parishes of the great South Side.*

Early in February the city of Chicago granted a permit for the parade. Or so we were led to believe.

Mayor Rahm had supported the idea in January but 19th Ward Alderman Matt O'Shea suddenly unleashed a full assault on the hopes and dreams of his wife's uncle, Skinny Sheahan. O'Shea contacted all his constituents condemning any talk of resurrection and sent a formal letter to the Mayor that included photos of debauchery from the '09 parade.

Suddenly the city was playing hardball in meetings with the parade committee and many wondered if the White House had stepped into the fray at the behest of the First Lady. What if the tales were true from Jody Kantor's book, "The Obamas" which stated, "...She (Michelle Obama), particularly resented the way power in Illinois was locked up generation after generation by a small group of families, all white Irish Catholic -- the Daleys in Chicago, the Hynes and Madigans statewide."

All of them Southside Irish.

Parade zealots became unhinged, declaring, "Of course, it's all part of their plan to diss the "breeders" and pro-life Catholics of the Southside by removing our ethnic identity and turning us all into socialist homosexual baby killers!"

City administrators scheduled a final showdown meeting with the parade committee for Friday, February 17th. Skinny flew back from vacation in Florida on the preceding Tuesday and that night he met at the Shamrock pub on Kinzie with Sun-Times Pulitzer Prize winning scribe Mark Konkol.

Bourbon Street would be hosting the big parade fundraiser that Saturday night and sponsors supposedly were getting spooked in fear of losing city contracts. The talk on the Southside was taking an ugly turn as the revival teetered in jeopardy. Neither Alderman O'Shea nor Skinny would budge and the fight had become even more than personal, extrapolating into a full-fledged family feud.

Skinny vented to Konkol that night and as he left I shouted across the bar to the reporter, "If you feck us, we'll never forget it!"

The stage was now set. The world awaited Friday the 17th.

The story hit the paper Friday morning, with a front-page teaser that said, "The Alderman VS. Uncle Skinny". Konkol showed us why he won the Pulitzer, with a summary of the facts that was evenhanded, fair, and above all, avoided any "scorched earth" rhetoric from anyone. It laid the groundwork for peace and that afternoon Skinny faced the cameras after meeting with the city and declared that the parade would indeed be back on Sunday March 11th. Alderman O'Shea magnanimously said, "I think it's going to happen, yeah."

Saturday night the fundraiser at Bourbon Street was packed to the rafters with Southsiders celebrating the return of the parade. The Sheahans and O'Sheas were family after all.

For those on the south side, the tradition has been restored. For those of us who left the Southside years ago, we will always have the parade to remind us of our Irish heritage, our parents and families, and the faith that guided us through all our troubles. Join us on parade day, Sunday March 11th, or better yet, volunteer today to help.

At the fundraiser there was talk that the opposition by Alderman O'Shea was a publicity stunt and he was in on it all along, wanting the parade back that he'd enjoyed for so many years as an organizer.

So was it a hoax? What's the truth?

Well, to paraphrase from one of my favorite movies, "The Man Who Shot Liberty Valance"—

*"This is the **Southside**, sir. When the legend becomes fact, print the legend."*

*   *   *

So now it's only three years since the parade has been resurrected and the 19th Ward, home to the parade, is divided in its choice for Mayor. And the factions backing Rahm are on edge with the prospect of an upstart Mexican unseating their clout. Rahm has made inroads to the unions and many of them have endorsed the Mayor for re-election. But not all of them.

And the rank and file union members we met with on Super Bowl Sunday were certainly anti-Rahm. At least they were back in February. Chuy had pushed the election to a run off and nerves were raw with emotion out there on the streets of the south side.

Today the old guard of the 19th Ward was standing with Rahm, whether reluctantly or not, there they were, kissing his ass on Western Avenue. 19th Ward Alderman Matt O'Shea was hosting the Mayor on his turf.

But Mike "Pickle" Joyce represented another faction and had his own base in the 19th Ward. Pickle had operated The Celtic Boxing Club for neighborhood kids for over 20 years. It was his group that Chuy would be marching with in the parade. Pickle's dad, Jeremiah Joyce, had also been 19th Ward Alderman as well as State Senator of this district representing the neighborhood. Pickle's brother Kevin had represented the 19th Ward in Springfield as a member of the General

Assembly. The Joyces were neighborhood guys, Irish and Catholic like St. Patrick. Chuy was a neighborhood guy and also Catholic like St. Patrick. Today there was a stark contrast between Chuy, who was clad in a Kelly green shamrock covered Celtic Boxing Club pullover and who fit in naturally with the crowd, and the Northside ballerina, who was wearing a green satin disco windbreaker.

It was a gorgeous day for a parade and Pickle had Chuckie B. drop me, Crawford and Cyril off at the float at 100th and Western. Pickle's wife Jamillah, daughter of the Greatest Heavyweight Champion of All Time, Muhammed Ali, was also on the float with her kids and her twin sister Rasheda, and their tacit endorsement on display as well, along with an Irish trio of guys playing tunes on the float.

We milled around until getting a phone call that told us that Chuy was going to be dropped off at 103rd and Western, kickoff point for the parade. Crawford, Cyril and I made our way down Western, heading south.

On the way we had to cross the paths of Rahm and the unions backing him, and the rest of his sycophants, as they milled around at their 102nd Street staging area. Many of those guys were our friends, some were not, particularly today.

I saw Mike Tierney in the crowd as I walked down the street and we exchanged begrudging glares. I could feel the hard-ass hate from members of Local 130, 399, and 150. Skinny Sheahan was there too, trying to keep his head down and out of the fight, known by some as "the Neville Chamberlin of the 19th Ward."

Chuy hops out of a black SUV at 103rd and comes over to us with his entourage of press folks and supporters. The media once again descends on him but for some reason, the kids handling Chuy feel the need to run down the street and away from the press. I think they've seen too many scenes of paparazzi chasing movie stars on TMZ. They get about fifty yards north on Western and I yell, "Stop, where the hell are you going? We want Chuy to talk to the press! We need the free media kids. So slow down. Talk to the media!"

Once Chuy talks to them for about fifteen minutes the interest dies down and we start walking to our float, in front of Town Liquors at

100th and Western. I bump into my old pal, Johnny Vegas Sheahan, the billboard king. Johnny has brought along several dozen green moustaches, and he hands me a couple. It's a great bit, especially with the moustache somehow becoming the logo for our mayoral candidate Jesus "Chuy" Garcia. I think Johnny was hoping to sell all the moustaches, but he decided to just start giving them away at this point.

I put one on and immediately turned to find Chicago Tribune columnist John Kass, walking with us to the float to interview Chuy. Kass had written several columns whacking Rahm and he was on our side. He took my picture with the stache and posted it on his website when the column was finished.

At this point I knew the Plumbers Union would be ready to crucify me.

Houli at the Southside Irish Parade, photo by John Kass.

The parade steps off and the crowd loves Chuy, once again chanting, "Chew-ey, Chew-ey, Chew-ey." It's a gorgeous day for a parade on the ol' Southside of Chicago and I am proud to be marching with Jesus.

Chuy continues to break from the middle to shake hands along the route, doing running high fives and shaking hands. It's a tremendous reception and then at 115th Chuy hustles to a waiting black SUV and takes off.

We're standing in front of the Beverly Woods and I turn to Crawford, "Well, let's get a drink!"

Inside the Sheahan family is hosting their annual post-parade party. They used to do it at Skinny's house and backyard, complete with Cook County jail bologna sandwiches in baggies to go along with your beer. But that was the good ol' days. Today it's free pizza and beer, thanks to the Sheahans.

As I come out of the john, I see Bill Gainer and Mike Tierney chewing on Skinny's ear about me. "You better tell him!"

I give them both the eyeball and ask Skinny what's up. He tells me, "They're saying we're gonna lose all our sponsors on the radio show because of you."

"Not all of them, just the pussies".

I walk into the party and grab a beer and some pizza and give the nod to Matt O'Shea and Crawford and I sit back and laugh. I send another text to Manny asking when the hell we are going to get our five grand? And my phone blows up, it's Manny!

"Would you guys be willing to take THREE grand?"

Ab-so-fuckin' lutely!

Monday, March 16, 2015
Chicagoland

Thirteen shootings today, with two homicides: Elijah Moore 41, and Deonte Jackson 34.

Mayoral Debate /Skinny & Houli Show

Okay, I go by the campaign office today and pick up our check and NO PROBLEM! The way I look at it, three in the hand was better than five we might not ever see. Crawford agreed. Hell he was getting a free ride, I think he only showed up at 10% of the events anyway.

Tonight we have scheduled a special taping of our radio show since Jimmy Deenihan, Ireland TD Minister for the Diaspora is in town for the parades and he is a good friend of The Skinny & Houli Show and whenever he is in town we have him on the show. Saw him at the Irish Fellowship dinner on Friday and came over to his table to remind him and he says, "Houli I wouldn't miss the opportunity to speak to the MILLIONS of listeners of the Skinny & Houli Show!"

Wise guy.

So I've got it all set up for 8:30 that night in the private party room of Lizzie McNeill's Irish Pub. Jimmy will be coming back from Milwaukee with Irish Consul General Aidan Cronin and they will hop in a cab to meet us for the show. Skinny and I have invited Bob Flood, our main sponsor of the show, along with his son Mike and a few other folks to meet the Minister at the taping. We have our own private bartender and we are all set.

I arrive a bit early. I usually gain entrance to the private party room by going through Lizzie's and entering behind the bar and walking thru the lobby of the building, getting on the elevator and up. But tonight there is a sign on the front door that says, PRIVATE PARTY, NO ADMITTANCE.

That's unusual I think and walk around instead to the entrance of the adjacent condo building. When I get upstairs and meet the bartender and our producer Billy Wooten, they inform me that the private party is a fundraiser for RAHM EMANUEL!

Holy shit, the devil in our midst!

So we're all up in the party room getting ready to tape the show, and Skinny is not here. I've got Black Dave Cahill from County Kerry, with his son George, and Bob and Mike Flood, Kevin Flood, and a handful of other Irishmen. Irish guys have a knack for colorful language, often times cussing and swearing at will, so I trot out one of my favorite jokes while we are waiting for the rest of our guests.

The nun was quizzing her students and asked them, "Who can use the word 'contagious' in a sentence?"

Suzy says, "Oh sister my little brother had measles and my mom kept him home from school and told me he was 'contagious.'"

Maeve yells out, "Sister, they wouldn't let my uncle on the plane when he had mumps cuz he was 'contagious'!"

Finally, little Jimmy says, "Sister, I was out in the back yard sittin' with me da, and the lady next door was painting her fence, and she had a huge fence and a little, tiny brush, and I asked me da, 'how long will it take her to paint that fence?'

And me da said, 'It'll take the cunt ages!'"

Finally, Consul General Aidan Cronin, and Minister for the Diaspora, Jimmy Deenihan show up from the train station and everybody is here but Skinny. I call him on the cell phone, where the hell are you? He says, "Is everybody there?"

Yeah, we gotta start without you, everybody is here!

"I'll be right up."

Okay, so now we know where he is, at Rahm Emanuel's feckin' fundraiser. We taped the show and Jimmy Deenihan was terrific, as always. It was a great show but that earlier event downstairs had left a creepy feeling in my stomach. But the show must go on!

First Debate

Tonight is the first one-on-one debate between Mayor Rahm and Chuy and our guy acquits himself well.

Watching the debate, Carol Marin is the moderator. Rahm says "property taxes are off the table", a lie. Chuy attacks- "The Mayor proposes corporate welfare for his cronies and rich friends . . . He promised to get the city's fiscal house in order four years ago and today we are in a financial crisis."

Rahm lies about how he has cut the deficit. Chuy attacks, "He underfunded the pension funds, he is part of the problem, he's giving tax breaks to the rich and wealthy."

Carol Marin starts attacking Chuy, she keeps cutting him off during talk of red light cameras, won't let him finish, then says to Rahm, "Go ahead Mayor" She is letting Rahm run the debate right now.

Red light cameras, Rahm blames Daley, "I inherited a corrupt system, threw the operator out." He throws out stats on 'safety' of red light cameras with a 3 second yellow light and other bullshit. Chuy says, "The cameras are a lie." It's all about the money.

They take questions from plants in the audience. Rahm is very glib, with stats and bullshit for each question, did he get them in advance?

They discuss the city's financial crisis, Rahm blames the pensions, Chuy says "You did nothing to change the financial situation." Rahm goes to blah blah stats.

Marin goes after Chuy, you owe the Chicago Teachers Union, how do you expect to negotiate with an even hand? Rahm says, "**I've made the CPS better while working with Barbara Byrd Bennett to extend the school day.**"

Uh, let's fast forward to learn that Barbara Byrd Bennett was sentenced April 28, 2017 to 4.5 years in prison on federal corruption charges. Byrd Bennett pleaded guilty two years ago to wire fraud. She admitted to steering more than $23 million in no-bid contracts to her former employer, in exchange for kickbacks.

Marin asks why is the city shrinking? Chuy says, "We haven't invested in the neighborhoods, most of Rahm's investments have been downtown for his rich friends." Rahm says we shouldn't pit one section of town against another and throws out more bs stats. Excuse me boys, but DUH, don't you think the city might be shrinking because every night dozens of people are SHOT walking down the street?

Marin finishes up the debate asking each guy for a ONE BIG IDEA for the city. Chuy sites the Port of Chicago and Rahm suggests the Chicago River as an economic engine. Marin says "Well those are very 'watery' big ideas"

Here's another big monumental idea, how about we STOP THE KILLING?

He does well, but sorry Chuy, you still sound like an immigrant with your slow, staccato style of speaking.

Two more debates scheduled before election day.

Tuesday March 17, 2015
Chicagoland

Only one shooting today, 25-year-old male in Humboldt Park.

St. Patrick's Day, Chuy visits the Irish American Heritage Center

I meet Chuy outside the Irish American Heritage Center around 4PM for a meet and greet. Chuy is feeling chipper after a more aggressive debate performance and I tell him, "Remember I told you to kick that guy in the balls? Last night you did. Keep doin' it."

There's a huge crowd of folks at the Center and Bob McNamara and the Chancey Brothers are playing onstage. McNamara makes an announcement to the crowd, "Folks we have a celebrity here today in our midst . . . (as everybody eyeballs Chuy) . . . give it up for Houli."

Pretty funny and even Chuy laughs. Folks are glad to meet him and we put him behind the bar to pour pints of Guinness as he was coached by bartender, Mark Hackett, from Drogheda, County Louth, Ireland.

Chuy pours a pint in The Fifth Province Pub
at the Irish American Heritage Center on St. Patrick's Day
with bartender Mark Hackett.
Photo courtesy of Gokhan Cukorova.

Wednesday March 18, 2015

Chuy heads to Los Angeles to raise dough.

Chuy went with some members of the campaign today to visit rich liberals in LA who might donate to the campaign. I doubt that anything will come of this. I think many of the goo-goo's working this campaign think they are working with Che Guevera to save the world or some such bullshit.

A new guy, David Keith, recently showed up with a few others, young guys in suits who seemed to have watched every episode of The West Wing. These mopes think it's all on the square.

Reminds me of "Radical Chic", when the Black Panthers would visit white liberal Jews to shake them down for money. They are actually participating in a very expensive "circle jerk".

Let's all stand around and tell each other how we are changing the world for the common man by drinking your booze and sucking each other's ballz.

Gimme a feckin' break, boys. This is an election for Mayor of Chicago, one of the largest cities in the world. If you want to find money, there is plenty of it right here in our backyard.

The campaign seems to be run without any plan whatsoever, just everybody slapping each other on the back and calling each other 'bro. No attack, just reacting to the daily slap from Rahm, the establishment, the ogre on the throne. Just keep chasing your tails boys.

Thursday March 19, 2015
Chicagoland

A dozen shootings today all over the city.

Friday March, 20, 2015

Four murders last night: Juan Warrior 43 in Chatham, James White 20 in Austin, Joseph Burdine 24 in Ashburn, and Fabian Echevarria 24 in West Town.

Last week the Service Employees International Union in Illinois finally endorsed Chuy. Today they unveiled their first TV commercial attacking Rahm in a scathing expose of his term and his tactics.

The SEIU spot opens with a shot of Chicago skyscrapers and the voice over says, "From up here, Chicago never looked better."

But then it cuts to a crime scene in the ghetto, "But down here, under Mayor Rahm Emanuel we've seen nearly 10,000 shootings, 50 neighborhood schools shut down, and a mayor who hits working people with higher taxes and fees, while giving special tax breaks to his friends at the very top. Now you see why they're spending millions falsely attacking Chuy Garcia. Because Rahm can't change his record, we need to change mayors."

I couldn't have said it better myself. It's a very effective slam on the Mayor telling it like it is: Rahm is bad for Chicago.

SEIU Local 1 represents janitors, the working people of our nation and they now see some daylight with this runoff election. The labor group has committed up to $2 million to Chuy's campaign. It couldn't have come at a better time.

Local 1 President Tom Balanoff is quoted in the paper, "We think there is a clear contrast between Chuy Garcia and Rahm Emanuel. Mayor Emanuel doesn't understand, that what made Chicago great was working people. We think he has totally turned his back on that."

Finally, somebody is saying it! Rahm is a bad actor.

Our TV commercials are total dog crap. Thankfully SEIU put together an attack ad that is very effective.

Here's my "call to arms" that I sent to deaf ears.

I talked to Mike Joyce today who tells me the campaign will not pay for a mailer to the black community. I'd like to go on record to say this is a mistake. Whatever money you have should be directed against Rahm through mailers or TV ads. You guys hired me to give you my input so as we hit the final week here's my take.

Our campaign is disorganized and without a clear message, doesn't return phone calls or follow up with key people, and yet in spite of that we appear to be at least in contention. That's a miracle in itself and I think it goes to the genuine "likeability" of our candidate.

I see articles in the New York Times and other communist outlets, which tout Chuy's ties to the left fringe of the Democratic Party as the reason for his success. I want to tell you that is complete bullshit and warn you that if Al Sharpton or Elizabeth Warren or any other wack job shows up to campaign for Chuy you can kiss your Irish vote, and almost any other white ethnic vote you have earned, goodbye. Play it straight and leave the ideological crap out of it. Chuy is the "neighborhood guy" who went to St. Rita, he is looking out for the little guy and is fighting the big money influences that have corrupted our city.

The SEIU TV commercial should be playing day and night. The message should be Rahm=bad, Chuy=good, it's as simple as that. Leave the nuance and phony fringe crap to the eggheads to eat that up, but your message should be good vs. evil. Everybody can understand that and they don't need a PHD to suss it out.

Don't fumble the ball on the goal line! Attack Rahm from every quarter and repeat over and over again that he is a liar and everything he says is a LIE!

And that's the truth!

Text from Schaffer:

Mike, are you free tonight for dinner with Chuy?
What time?
8PM Cocktails 8:30 Dinner
Les Nomades 222 E
Ontario. Jacket and tie
Okay see you then.

I call Pickle, he is going with his pal Calvin, will meet me there. He then tells me he thinks Andrew Sharp is a spy in the campaign and he is going to confront him tonight.
Looking forward to this dinner.
So I arrive on time, valet park it, very fancy shmancy French

restaurant, and we are in a private room upstairs. I order a beer and
shoot the breeze with Pickle and Calvin and Schaffer. They've invited
some big money guys to pitch for donations, can't remember their
names, but I told them we've had over ten thousand shootings in the
city and it's time for a new mayor. The guy seemed incredulous.

So I sit down at a table with Schaeffer and David Keith and a couple
of other new suits who all are working on their West Wing look. One
guy knows my niece who also works in politics, with the Democrats.

Waiter puts a shallow bowl in front of me and it looks like a little
pool of spit, couldn't have been more than a half a mouthful of some
"soup". I ask the table, 'what the hell is this? Is this soup?'

Schaffer says, "It's the starter, it's fine." Then he asks me to sit at
the table with the rich guys and Chuy. Okay, I sit down and order
another beer. I overhear Schaffer tell the waiter, "Keep the bottles of
wine coming."

Chuy is with his lovely wife, Evelyn, a very refined lady, and I'm
making small talk at the table. Next thing I know it's over and where
the hell is Pickle?

He tells me later that he asked Andrew Sharp to step outside for a
discussion where he put it to him. "Are you a spy for Rahm?"

Pickle tells me later, "I called him out, and he is full of shit."

I had been wondering about Andrew Sharp myself before this
and a few nights back had googled him to see if I could discover his
modus operandi.

I came upon a great story on an unverifiable news site, Chicago
News Bench, with the headline, BIZARRE ENCOUNTER WITH
ANDREW SHARP. It was written anonymously, of course, by
somebody who goes by the name 'RPB', short for Rogers Park Bench,
and the story laid out a scenario where Sharp is a nefarious political
operative out of Alexandria, Virginia who is lurking around the 49th
Ward on the north side, going by the name of "Seamus", and putting
on a phony Irish accent. It sounded like he scared RPB., which was
funny to me because I found Sharp to be about as scary as Mr. Rogers.

I passed the item on to Pickle and he got even more suspicious. If
Sharp was double dealing, Pick would smoke him out.

Pickle brought his pal Calvin Hollins with him to the meeting that night. Hollins is a black businessman in Chicago, heavily connected in the nightclub/entertainment scene here. Calvin got Halle Berry her start in show biz and knows all the big hitters, Michael Jordan, Oprah, celebrities, sports figures, politicians, you name it.

Pickle says, *"So Calvin was helping me out, on the campaign, in the black community, and with some people in the business community, Calvin is like a chameleon, he knows probably more white people than I do, but he's also somebody who is held in high regard in the black community."*

Calvin has a large group of well-heeled donors waiting in the wings to make a drop on Chuy, but he wants to make sure everything is legit.

But Pickle had smelled a rat when he saw the first TV spot the campaign put together for Chuy. It looked unprofessional, covered no new ground, and the opposition seemed to be expecting it.

That night of the fancy dinner at Les Nomades, Andrew Sharp ducked out early and Pickle and his pal Calvin followed him down the stairs and outside. Pickle stopped Sharp, "Hey I gotta talk to you"

Sharp excused himself, said his wife was waiting for him.

Pickle said, *"She can wait."*

With Calvin by his side, Mike Joyce cornered the campaign manager Andrew Sharp.

Sharp said, "Wha wha what's up?"

Pickle said, "I think you're a Quisling."

Vidkun Quisling, was a Norwegian who collaborated with the Nazis in World War II. His name has become synonymous with traitors, equivocators, and scoundrels ever since.

But Sharp is not that sharp, and said, "What's that?"

Pickle enlightened him, *"I think you're a spy, an insider."*

A mole.

Sharp was flummoxed. "What?" "Why do you say that?"

Mike "Pickle" Joyce then laid it all out for him: the commercial, the issue, the cheap filmmaking technique.

Sharp countered, "Oh, that's a legitimate issue . . . we did that so the commercial would have an 'urban feel' to it."

Pickle says, *"Why did you do this commercial and three hours later, Rahm has a rebuttal commercial up with Carol Marin, Mike Flannery and Chuy's own words contradicting the commercial that Chuy put up?"*

Sharp's answer is almost laughable. "Well . . . they've got a quick turnaround time."

*"Yeah, real quick, if you're **tellin' em**."*

Pickle had done some digging and discovered that Sharp had worked in his past with other Democratic consultants who were tight with Rahm.

Denmark was starting to stink.

Pickle can be an intimidating character. He's a former professional boxer and coach and standing next to him in the street is this mysterious black guy, Calvin. And it's a Friday night in Chicago.

Pickle is eyeballing Sharp, who looks like he has just seen a ghost.

He tells me, "I was terrified that Sharp was feeding Rahm's campaign inside dope."

Pickle looks at Sharp and says, "Bullshit . . . Calvin has a lot of people from the community on the line and if we find out you're not on the square, they're gonna hold you responsible, just so ya' know. And then me and Calvin left."

I can sense Pickle becoming disillusioned with the campaign. They don't want to pay for his mailer to the black community. They don't have their shit together and he knows it. I'm thinking maybe he is just becoming paranoid, but who knows? Lots of new faces around all of a sudden, is that where the money is going?

Saturday March 21, 2015

Chicagoland

Nine shootings today, two homicides: Alexander Colon 22, shot in the chest in Gresham and Delia Colunga 23 white female, shot in the head on East Side.

Sunday March 22, 2015
Chicagoland

Eleven shootings today, one murder: Dushante Hassell 21 shot in the head in Lincoln Square.

Pickle forwards a text to me that he sent to Chuy today.

Chuy, tomorrow starts early voting and we still have no campaign lit, signs, or list of volunteers, coordination or cooperation. What I have been given is evasive answers, empty promises, excuses and outright lies. I am willing to give it my all, but I can't go to war with no weapons, and I certainly can't ask people willing to help to walk the plank. The latest polls show you trailing by 16 points and I realize that is not accurate, but barring a major wakeup, that poll will serve as a self-fulfilling prophesy. Please advise as nobody in the campaign seems to have the ability nor the inclination to make a decision.

Monday March 23, 2015
Chicagoland

Six shootings today.

Tuesday, March 24, 2015
Chicagoland

Six shootings, one homicide: Anthony Hayes, 17, murdered in Garfield Park.

Thursday, March 26, 2015
Chicagoland

Seven shootings last night, one homicide: Edgar Muneton 25, shot in the stomach in Belmont Cragin.

Second Debate between Chuy and Rahm

This debate is on Fox 32, WFLD and political reporter Mike Flannery is the moderator. The night I saw this I thought Flannery was kissing up to Rahm but on second look, he was just trying to get his licks in on both of them. I'm not sure what exactly the role of a moderator is. Should they be calling bullshit on the candidates when they lie or just setting them up for statements? Still not sure.

CPS has a billion-dollar deficit; Flannery asks if there is going to be another school teacher strike. Rahm says No. Chuy says, "Four years ago this Mayor said he would make it (the school system) better, today it's worse. He *appointed* the leadership." Makes oblique reference to Barbara Byrd Bennett profiting from connections while on the CPS board.

Flannery to Chuy, "You are connected to Karen Lewis of the CTU (Chicago Teachers Union)."

Rahm says of Chuy, "All he's done is attack.", blames pensions again, once again he's very glib.

Every time Rahm gestures with his right hand you notice the missing finger. There is something demonic about it. And what is the deal with Mike Flannery's "business beard"? He's got a moustache and then this very thin beard, almost just a Nixonian five o'clock shadow, you wanna say, make up your mind, either grow the beard or don't for cripes sakes. The beard can't hide the fact that you are bald, no matter how subtle you groom it pal.

Rahm spouts more slick stats, and then says, "My opponent disagreed with a full school day." Chuy laughs, "No I don't, you're lying again!" Good stuff.

Flannery says, "Let the mayor finish." Rahm is boasting about how great the Chicago Public School system is these days, makes it sound like Harvard instead of the cesspool it actually is.

Flannery says, "We're gonna switch gears now", and accuses Chuy of not endorsing the Obama library, "What were you thinking?"

Oh yes, let's all get down on our knees and kiss the ass of the worst President this country has ever had, and the biggest killer of babies in the last eight years thanks to his pals at Planned Parenthood. Makes me puke. Chuy says he only was against it because they wanted to put it on park district land.

Flannery says, "What about the Lucas library?"

Chuy says, "You mean the museum?"

Star Wars creator George Lucas wanted to build his spaceship on the lake front and Rahm was trying to "Rahm" that through for his Hollywood pals.

Chuy disagrees, "You're not the king of this city!"

Rahm says, "It's all about leadership, I am consistent."

If you mean consistently an asshole, then yes.

I'll say this about Rahm, he is a very good bullshitter. He makes these pronouncements and if you didn't know better, you might buy it. Like him taking credit for shutting down a coal plant in Chuy's own neighborhood of Little Village. Chuy is so flabbergasted by this lie that he laughs again. "You singlehandedly closed it? People were working on getting that plant closed for over twenty years!"

Chuy is aghast at Rahm's audacious boast. "Before Mayor Emanuel moved to Chicago, the people of Little Village were protesting that coal plant. The park he claims credit for? He simply showed up there to cut the ribbon! He's grand standing, trying to take credit for what others have done!"

This debate is a battle, Chuy is holding his own against the facile downright falsity of Rahm's claims. They cover lots of ground that bore me, taxes, bike lanes, pensions again, Rahm obliquely blames the Daleys, and then finally we get to the elephant in the room: crime.

Chuy says, "We've had over ten thousand shootings, almost two thousand homicides. The most important role of the mayor is to provide for the pubic safety of the citizens."

That's my takeaway folks. Bottom line, what good are bike lanes, tax relief, or any of this other bullshit, if they are shooting at you?

At one-point Mike Flannery turned to Chuy and said, "What does that mean when you say the mayor is not for the neighborhoods? Is it because he went to high school in the suburbs? Is that bad? Does that mean he should not be mayor?"

YES!

Chuy says, "The mayor doesn't listen to people, he doesn't engage them in a natural fashion. It's all about the press releases, taking credit for things he didn't do, like he just did! He's not rooted in the day-to-day life of the Chicago community."

I think that says it all. Reminds me of my old pal from Bridgeport, Dr. Ronnie, remarking about a guy we knew who was somewhat Rahmesque, when he said, "Too much college, not enough high school."

Chuy won this debate, hands down.

Friday, March 27, 2015

Chicagoland

Seven shootings, one homicide: Uchena Agina 24 shot in the head in Avalon Park.

We started early this morning out in Beverly at the train station at 103rd and Longwood. Most of us met up with Pickle at the Starbucks on the corner there. The plan was a meet and greet with commuters from all over Beverly area to shake hands with Chuy.

Lots of photos of this, but not a lot of people. I've never seen Beverly so deserted.

Chuy at Rock Island train station.
Photo courtesy of Mike Houlihan

We drove Chuy around to Mt. Greenwood polling place, Top Notch, train stations, Keane gas station, which had just been robbed a few days earlier. I told the two guys working there, "You won't get robbed when Chuy is mayor!"

We took Chuy over to the Mt. Greenwood polling place at the park on 111th Street, nobody there, except the two Chicago Park District workers, who were absolutely blown away that Chuy was there. Took a photo with them too.

Chuy with Chicago Park District guys.
Photo courtesy of Mike Houlihan.

Somehow on this Friday morning, Beverly had turned into a ghost town.

Pickle's sister in law, Rasheda Ali, was in town later today to do a press conference to endorse Chuy.

I talked to Pickle later in the day, he was kinda crazed. He talks so fast when he is stressed, his mouth can't keep up with his mind.

He's talking about three things at once, not making sense, running on no sleep. I finally ask him, what the hell is wrong with you?

"My mother's in the hospital."

His mom had fallen and broken her leg and Mike was worried about her.

Saturday, March 28, 2015

Chicagoland

Ten shootings today, two murders: Michael Ricks, 36, shot in the stomach at 22nd and Michigan, and Quentin A. Thompson, 26, shot in the head in Chatham.

Chuy headed over to Rainbow Push Headquarters today to try to psych up the troops with Jesse Jackson. Cyril Regan told me later, he was doing assist on the event, got there before Chuy and walked up the aisle and on to the stage to check the microphones. He turns around at the podium and the audience bursts into applause. They thought Cyril was Chuy! Just another white guy with a moustache! Except this one has an Irish brogue.

Pickle called me, in a good mood, sounds like he got some rest because I could actually understand what he was saying.

"I feel good, I'm on the front page of the Sun-Times tomorrow, some bullshit about revenge."

A smear campaign, you can see the hand of Rahm behind it, he uses the Sun-Times to smear his enemies.

Was it Sneed?

"No it was that Novak."

The article said they had attempted to reach him, but "they never called me."

"It got some of our people fired up, they've been pulling down Chuy signs in front of the Mt. Greenwood park polling place. Chuckie B is gonna get some people and go over there, most of them are teachers who are strong behind Chuy and cops who hate Rahm."

The Chuy campaign didn't have anyone manning <u>any</u> of the early polling places in the city. Go figure that out.

In the 19th Ward, the early voting polling place was Mt. Greenwood Park. On the last weekend of early voting, the week before the election, flyers were posted around the hood, with notices in the Beverly Review and on the Patch, saying "Come join us at TRs for a pre-election rally and a day of early voting with Rahm Emanuel and local union leaders and members of organized labor".

TR's is a local tavern almost directly across 111th Street from Mount Greenwood Park, where early voting was taking place. Throughout the early voting period Chuy campaign signs had been mysteriously disappearing from in front of the polling place.

This is an old game in Chicago politics, but it sometimes can turn nasty.

Friday night before the Rahm rally at TR's, some of Chuy's guys put up some signs and by Saturday they were gone.

On Saturday a group of female teachers from the neighborhood, Chicago Public School Teachers CTU, young women whose union was strongly behind Chuy Garcia, volunteered to work the early voting polling place at Mt. Greenwood Park on that Saturday, for the last day of early voting

Saturday morning, they put the Chuy signs in front and in back of the Rahm signs, basically making 'sandwiches' out of the Rahm signs.

Saturday at noon, before the rally, a handful of Rahm-supporting union guys, walked across the street and started giving the girls shit about being there.

Our old pal, Chuckie B., and a couple of off-duty Chicago police officers, stepped out of their cars at this point and with their best Southside chivalry said, "You guys got a problem?"

This is right on 111th street, in front of Mt. Greenwood park. The union guys moseyed back across the street and never even came back to vote.

Rahm's people did not get the photo op they wanted, "early voting by union members". They just stayed in the bar.

When Rahm showed up at TR's the union guys, who were mostly city workers, just kept drinking their free tap beer and watching the game on the tube while Rahm gave another speech while pissing into the wind. If Chuy was there, they'd have called it a "Mexican Stand-Off"!

People forget that Chuy had some pretty impressive union support of his own. The Amalgamated Transit Union locals, the Service

Employees International Union's Illinois State Council and, best of all, the Chicago Teachers Union.

I went out to get the Sunday edition of the Sun-Times. Pickle had soft pedaled it but it turned out to be a front page smear of Pickle and his entire family. The Rahmfather's connections to the Sun-Times are pretty well known so it didn't come as much of a surprise. The owners of the paper had all donated significant bucks to their pal, Rahm. Most of the staff at the Sun-Times are goo-goo's.

I worked there for three years, freelancing, most of the writers there hated me, especially the women. I guess it was because I'm a racist, homophobic, misogynist, etc. Yeah, yeah, yeah.

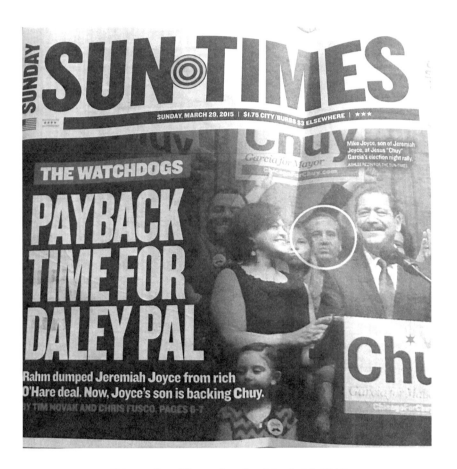

Chicago Sun-Times, Sunday March 29, 2015
From Chicago Sun-Times, (March 29) ' (2015) Sun-Times Media.
All rights reserved. Used by permission and protected by the
Copyright Laws of the United States. The printing, copying,
redistribution, or retransmission of this Content,
without express written permission is prohibited.

They had used the election night photo of Chuy and Pickle, (from the night we forced the ballerina into a runoff), on the front page for their big expose, written by The Watch Dogs.

"The Watch Dogs"-yeah, they are dogs in that they are chasing their tails and want to lick their own ballz. What a joke. Supposedly Pickle was working for Chuy because his old man had lost a contract at O'Hare years ago. Don't know how that is a story, regardless of his motives.

My original motive was money, obviously, but I had grown so irritated with Rahm's style and his Clintonian tactics that I wanted to crush this little reptile with my bare hands. I like a good fight, a fair fight, but I also like to see bullies get their nutsacks handed to them in the end.

As my wife had said the night before, "This is just personal for you now." She was right of course, my motives had been perverted not by money, but by wanting to do the right thing. This guy is bad for Chicago, from every perspective.

I felt bad for Pickle, not because he would suffer because of the false innuendo and lies of the front page smear story, but because I know him to be a good hearted guy who sincerely wants to help people in his community. He likes a fight too, that's why he's devoted so many years to coaching black kids as boxers and showing them a better way up and out of the hood.

Ten days to the election, but this put a very bad taste in my mouth.

*   *   *

Palm Sunday, March 29, 2015
Chicagoland

Three shootings including the murder of Ronnie Finch, 25, who was shot in the head in West Pullman.

Bob Fioretti endorses Rahm.

Cyril and I were scheduled today to staff the Greek Parade down Halsted Street. Chuy was the "honorary" Grand Marshall. When the campaign told me he was going to be Grand Marshall I thought wow, how did he ace out some Greek for that position. Turns out he didn't, there were about a dozen honorary guys.

It's not much of a parade and while we're lining up I ask Chuy if he's seen today's Sun-Times featuring our pal Pickle on the front page.

Chuy says, "Well he had to know that was coming!"

The big news is of course Fioretti endorsing Rahm today, at a press conference scheduled for later in the day. I figure they must have paid him off, he probably had campaign debts, and he just came off a bout with cancer etc. But I knew Bob was pretty much ending his political career with the endorsement, because he had spent years fighting Rahm in the City Council and now they were all calling Fioretti "Judas", and on Palm Sunday too!

Pickle told me Fioretti had approached the Chuy campaign and all he wanted was a commitment to help him with his campaign debt if Chuy won, but they would not pay. Pick also told me Fioretti had called him on Friday, but he never called him back. Who knows the real truth? Not me, this whole thing has turned into a Jabberwocky with dozens of duplicitous characters. As for me, I just want to hang on to see Rahm defeated, and get a nice cushy job from Chuy as the Commissioner of Irish Relations or some bullshit like that.

After the parade I call William Kelly on my cell phone. Kelly was an early candidate and avid attacker of Rahm. Kelly's PAC has produced the best anti-Rahm TV commercial of the campaign. When I tell him Fioretti is endorsing Rahm, he is stunned and wants to know where and when the press conference will be held. Kelly tells me he wants to run over there and disrupt it. Well good luck with that Wild Bill, but I think you might be too late.

Headed home not sure where this thing is heading, but definitely enjoying the chaos.

Monday March 30, 2015
Chicagoland

Nine victims today, including Keith Stokes, 24, shot in the chest and murdered in Englewood.

Chuy is speaking today at the City Club of Chicago.
This is from their website:

*The City Club of Chicago is a non-profit, **non-partisan organization** whose members include prominent business, civic and government leaders in Chicago. The organization attracts those interested in civic responsibility, public issues, open political debate and networking opportunities. Founded in 1903, it is the longest-running civic forum in Chicago.*

The mission of the City Club of Chicago is to provide a forum for the discussion of civic and public affairs in Chicago, the metropolitan area and the State of Illinois.

The City Club is run by my pal Jay Doherty, who was and still is the Kennedy family guy in Chicago. It's held at Maggiano's restaurant, the food is great, and the discussions are mostly great. They claim to be non-partisan. Rahm is a regular guest spouting his bullshit and the moderator was usually the late, political professor Paul Green. The same Paul Green who got so bent out of shape at me taking my slap at Rahm when publicizing the party for Chuy at O'Rourke's office on Western Avenue when Obama and Rahm took over Pullman back in February.

They regularly feature newsworthy politicians pitching their platforms. Looks like they waited til the last minute to invite Chuy Garcia, one week before the election, but better late than never.

Crawford and I are all set to go but when we get there we discover there is a fee. Contemplating a way to sneak in, I call Skinny, hoping to avoid this. He's a City Club member and he won't be there today so do me a favor. He does, puts me in touch with a guy named "Tweed", and we take Skinny's seats for the day.

Me and Crawford are feeling pretty good in spite of the polls putting Chuy behind. Primarily because we've been paid already, and in spite of everything the mood of the campaign is pretty positive. I've even talked them into an ad in the April issue of the Irish American News and they paid that too!

I saw Paul Green beforehand and I'm wary of how he's going to treat our guy. He's the moderator and can set you up with the wrong question, which are submitted by audience members during the speech. Crawford and I say hello to Chuy and I lean in and tell him, "Watch out for that guy Green, he's not on your side."

We take our seats at a table with some folks from the campaign, including sitting City Clerk and former Mayor David Orr. He's a supporter of Chuy and was mayor of Chicago for like five minutes back in the eighties when Harold Washington died. Orr was vice mayor when Harold croaked, but the city council selected the late, great, Eugene Sawyer in a midnight massacre over the Thanksgiving holiday weekend as thousands of black demonstrators protested in the lobby of City Hall. That was a helluva night, the pinnacle and nadir of Chicago politics all at once.

In spite of his brief tenure, Orr's portrait hangs in the gallery of Chicago Mayors on the fifth floor in City Hall. It stands today as a testament to his tenacity as a whiner, according to the Inc column of the Tribune back in April of 1988.

The food is great, and Chuy gives his speech and the q&a is uneventful. It's an underwhelming performance and Crawford and I top it off across the street with a couple of pops at Fado Irish Pub.

Election day is a week from tomorrow.

Tuesday, March 31, 2015
Chicagoland

Susan Magiao-Watson, 52, white female, stabbed to death in Avondale.

Third and Final Debate Tonight-WTTW Studios, Phil Ponce is the moderator, presented by The City Club of Chicago

Phil Ponce is the moderator, a Latino, so you think we might have a chance. But it turns out he and Rahm are neighbors, live on the same block in Ravenswood. He has several sons who also work in Chicago television. Of course that's nepotism, but it's okay cuz it's not government. This guy makes Cook County Assessor Joe Berrios look like a piker.

There's a studio audience of combined Rahm and Chuy supporters and Ponce opens with "Let's get to it."

He asks Rahm about the city wanting to borrow $500 million to keep things going in this dire state of affairs. Rahms says, "I inherited this." Starting to sound like a broken record. Rahm says he can solve this with 3 options: progressive sales tax, casinos, and TIFs. It's all double talk. He says Chuy wants to "take reform off the table", blames career politicians kicking the can down the road.

Chuy says Rahm has already borrowed $1.7 billion, that's not good. Chuy wants a luxury tax on expensive stuff.

Ponce attacks Chuy for his leadership of Enlace. The organization was originally called the Little Village Community Development Corp. It grew quickly in its first several years under Garcia, but it suffered a financial crisis when the recession hit in 2008. Ponce puts up a screen shot of their last IRS Form 990, which lists a year end deficit. This is part of Rahm's playbook, they've been doing commercials about the alleged mismanagement while Chuy was in charge and accusing him of being unfit to be mayor because of his tenure with Enlace.

Chuy calls bullshit and says of Rahm, "He's trying to destroy the record of a non-profit."

Ponce pounces on Chuy's promise to appoint a commission to fix the city's financial problems. "Who will be on the commission? Who else?"

Ponce grills Chuy while Rahm pulls out his copy of the 990 form and waves it around.

Chuy fires back that everything was fine until Rahm and his pals at Freddie Mac caused the recession.

Rahm gets cute, "Only you and my mother think I singlehandedly started the recession!"

Rahm again proclaims "I didn't start the recession!", to laughter from the crowd, then rattles off some of his "accomplishments", including working with President Obama to turn the country around, a couple three other BS items and ends with "AND the number one Little League team in America!"

Applause from the crowd. Of course he's referring to the Jackie Robinson Little League Champs, who it later was revealed ***cheated by loading ringers onto the roster of the team and were disqualified for cheating by Little League.***

Rahm says Chuy is out of his league running for mayor, based on his tenure as leader of Enlace and implies Chuy doesn't have the chops to do the job, basically the same message he's been hitting in his TV spots for the last couple weeks to the tune of millions in air time. Rahm has been spending his $30 million bucks to buy TV time painting Chuy as just a dumb Mexican.

Rahm says Chuy has been promising all these gifts like he's "Hanuka Harry". Ponce jumps into the attack and as soon as Chuy starts to speak, says "Let the Mayor respond!"

I start to wonder if Chuy is sick. He looks very tired and his energy is low and he might have a touch of the flu, bad time to get it. Hope it wasn't from The Polar Plunge.

Ponce asks Chuy, "Is the city cooking the books?"

Well of course they are, they've been rigging not only finances but crime stats as well.

Chuy says, "There is a veiled secrecy and you can't get information about where the revenues are going in the city of Chicago. There is 'secrecy' in the finances. I want to open the books!"

But Chuy is on the ropes.

Ponce continually interrupts Chuy, then brings up O'Hare and the noise and the FAA. Zzzzzzzzzz

Ponce is a moron. What the feck are you asking him this shit for when there have been ten thousand kids shot? Many of those kids are Hispanic, like you Phil Ponce.

Chuy starts slapping Rahm around about not meeting with the families living by the airport and Rahm once again starts talking about how he shut down the coal plant in Little Village and once again taking credit for it and the park that was built there.

Ponce turns on Rahm suddenly, "Are you pay to play?"

The Tiny Dancer dances around it and calls Chuy a "career politician." Irony!

And this is where everything starts going south.

Rahm brings up the Palm Sunday front page story in the Sun-Times, the smear of the Joyce family and in particular one Michael Joyce.

I'm watching this at home and pick up the phone to text Pickle, as I hear Chuy say, "That's a lie!"

Texts with Pickle

"They are talking about you"!

"Who"?

"Phil Ponce and Rahm."

"What did they say?"

"Aren't you watching it?"

"No I am out. What did they say?

"Well expect phone calls, they brought up the Sun-Times story, Rahm trashed the Joyce family.

Debate is a mess!"

I call the Pick after these texts are exchanged. He and his wife Jamillah are out having dinner with Father George Clements and Father Dan Malette. I tell him to get to a TV as fast as possible.

*   *   *

Rahm started this with, "And just Sunday, the Chicago Sun-Times noted that the Joyce family, that I threw out of the airport for ten years having a no bid contract-is one of his biggest supporters in the campaign and they're running . . ."

Chuys says, "That's a lie!"

Ponce then jumps in: "One of the Joyce family members was standing right behind you at the podium on your election night . . ."

Chuy: "Okay what kind of donation has he made to the campaign? The fact that one person in one part of the city, one of 50 wards, wants to volunteer for me? That makes him a big donor? That's false!

Has he given me a thousand dollars? No.

He (Rahm) has received, according to Forbes magazine, over 20 million dollars from 100 donors! And they are all rich and powerful! When you have forces like that involved in politics, what happens to the little guy? What happens to taxpayers in the city of Chicago? They get shut out!

You (Rahm) buy the airwaves, you monopolize the discourse, you get your way!

He (Rahm) never thought he would be here tonight!"

Rahm rattles off, "Two things, one, you just called the Sun-Times liars for their cover page and two, Mr. Joyce was with you on your election night . . ." He's dancing like crazy now, dancing and denying, pontificating with phony facts about all the cranes he has brought to the skyline and Ponce tries to square things with this- "Mr. Mayor you received a $250,000 donation from Magic Johnson after one of his companies got an 80-million-dollar contract with the CPS? Is this another example of one of your contributors benefitting from a city deal?"

Rahm says "No, first of all . . . blah blah blah."

But Chuy is still pissed: "I have 6,000 volunteers on my campaign and he plucks one name who hasn't made any significant contribution to my campaign."

Ponce pivots, "Has he (Pickle) discussed getting contracts with you?

Chuy- "No, he's discussed getting votes in the 19th Ward, where he lives!"

And now things get really, really ugly.

Phil Ponce turns on fellow Latino Jesus Chuy Garcia and says "Your son has been arrested numerous times and court records describe him as a gang member . . . **If you can't keep your own son out of a gang, how can you steer the city away from gangs and violence?**"

There are audible gasps from the crowd. Rahm jumps at the opportunity to grandstand, scrunching his face into his best mask of compassion, "Can I say one thing? I don't think this is a fair line of questioning."

He probably wrote the fecking question himself and passed it to Ponce as they walked their poodles in Ravenswood this morning. Pure puke.

The audience applauds, just what Rahm was going for. Ponce doubles down, "If you can't keep your own son out of a gang how can you . . ." and the audience starts **booing** him.

Ponce says, to the audience, "Excuse me?" And continues with the question.

I text Pickle, with no response.

The audience is booing Phil Ponce! Phil Ponce should be hung by his balls!

*   *   *

It's a bad night for WTTW, (Wilmette talks to Winnetka), and all their goo-goo subscribers. Ponce shows himself to be pond scum and to do that to a fellow Latino makes it even more reprehensible.

The debate wraps up five minutes later and I'm in shock. Pickle has to call a press conference, RIGHT NOW! I call him and leave a message and start banging out a press release with a statement. It's only eight o'clock, figured I could drive to his house and be there by 8:45PM. I text him again

Text to Pickle

Definitely make a statement.

If you could call a nine thirty press conference you can make the ten pm news!

*   *   *

But Pickle is not biting. At least not tonight.

*   *   *

Pickle sent me an email around 9:30PM tonight with his statement and it gets posted on The 19th Ward Blog two days later.

Wednesday April 1, 2015

Chicagoland

Ten victims, nine shot including Dylane Hall, 16, shot in the back in Chicago Lawn, and Joyce Terrell, 27, stabbed to death in South Shore.

Lots of fallout about Ponce attacking Chuy during the debate. Just shows how the media is all in the tank for Rahm. But to have a Latino trying to sandbag the potential first Latino Mayor of Chicago was really low. Once again it's revealed that Phil Ponce lives just a few doors down from Rahm in Ravenswood. He's just another Chicagoan trying to protect his clout.

My April column in The Irish American News came out today, should put a target on my back for sure.

Here it is:

Irish American News April 2015

Hooliganism by Mike Houlihan

After watching the mayoral race for the last six weeks, I wish St. Patrick could jump forward in a time machine and rid us of the reptiles in Chicago politics.

He wasn't the most articulate dude in the bunch, but I think Dr. Willie Wilson got it right when he called an opponent, "an old snake in a new skin."

On Tuesday April 7th Chicago will make a decision between the "devil we know" and Jesus Chuy Garcia.

How do you feel after four years of watching a generation of young black men murder each other, as well as innocent kids, just standing on the corner? How do you feel about the school closings and teacher strikes and crooked crime stats? Rigged red light cameras and soaring water bills?

Do you think it's going to get any better? Are you scared? You should be.

"There is a tide in the affairs of men,

Which, taken at the flood, leads on to fortune,

Omitted, all the voyage of their life

Is bound in shallows and in miseries.

On such a full sea are we now afloat,

And we must take the current when it serves,

Or lose our ventures."

Maybe it's time to saddle up, like the Saint Patrick's battalion in the Mexican American War of 1846-48, Los San Patricios. They were mostly Irishmen who had fled the famine in Ireland, came to America and suffered anti-Catholic bigotry in the US Army. They heard the bells of the Angelus calling them to fight for Mexico and they defected. They heard the words of their leader, John Riley, when he told them, "A more hospitable and friendly people than the Mexican there exists not on the face of the earth . . . especially to an Irishman."

I met Chuy Garcia on Super Bowl Sunday as he hit fourteen bars in a record-breaking blizzard, campaigning up and down Western Avenue. He proudly wore his St. Rita Mustang hoodie and wherever we went Chicago Irish men and women warmly welcomed him.

I'm a pretty good judge of character. I can spot a phony at fifty yards and my BS detector is a finely tuned instrument of discernment. This guy is an honest and honorable hombre.

Chuy wants what's best for Chicago, not the ruling class.

Skeptics may scoff but I like to think of the words of the late, great Irish poet Seamus Heaney.

History says, don't hope

On this side of the grave.

But then, once in a lifetime

The longed-for tidal wave

Of justice can rise up,

And hope and history rhyme.

So hope for a great sea-change

On the far side of revenge.

Believe that further shore

Is reachable from here.

Believe in miracle

And cures and healing wells.

Sure it's a long shot, but in a fight like this, my money is always gonna be on the guy named Jesus. Please vote for Chuy Garcia on Tuesday April 7th.

Thursday April 2, 2015
Chicagoland

Ten people shot, including the murders of Charles Gray, 36, in Englewood, and Juan Simpson, 36, shot in the back in Grand Crossing.

CHICAGO (WLS) – Fioretti in hospital.

Ald. Bob Fioretti has been hospitalized with flu-like symptoms and a fever, a spokesperson said.

Fioretti went to Northwestern Memorial Hospital Tuesday and has been undergoing tests since then, officials said. He will remain in the hospital for more observation.

Fioretti finished fourth in the February mayoral election and this past weekend endorsed Mayor Rahm Emanuel for re-election.

Pickle's March 31st email to me was posted today on The 19th Ward Blog, with the following intro from "Murph the 4th", the blogger:

A letter from Pickle Joyce in response to the Rahm/Suntimes attack.

"You will never ever see a letter like this from any of these other elected or appointed, past or present public officials. Why? Because they can't write it. It would be bullshit.

This beautifully sums up some of the reasons we live here and why a vote for Chuy is really an endorsement of our values. It is a vote for a continuation of our lifestyle, here in the 19th ward."—Murph the 4th.

A letter from Pickle Joyce in response to the Rahm/Suntimes attack.

Don't shed any tears for me on the Sun Times smear piece done on me yesterday. I'm a big boy I can handle it. Rahm's got to be pretty desperate for me to rate the front page on a weekend where dozens of people were shot. For the record I was never contacted for comment on the article. If I had been contacted I would have informed them that I have worked on over 30 elections since Emanuel became mayor and that revenge and my family members were not pertinent to my support of Chuy Garcia. I am very proud of all of my family members and when somebody in the neighborhood is looking for help they are always there for them. As an elected official my father worked harder and did more for the residents of the 19th Ward than anybody. He did his job tirelessly, selflessly and didn't seek credit or publicity for serving his constituents. He was personally responsible for appointing Mike Sheahan, Ginger Rugai and Tom Dart to their first public offices. My brother Kevin was elected and served the residents of the 19th Ward as an Illinois State Representative. Kevin is a cancer survivor and is now the Vice President of Ave Maria University in Florida. Both my father and my brother were personally and politically pro-life Democrats. There has been nobody in Illinois politics that has been more pro-union than my father or my brother. As far as my involvement with Chuy Garcia goes, I became acquainted with Chuy Garcia through my good friend in the boxing business JC. JC's father and Chuy brought the great labor leader Cesar Chavez to Chicago over 30 years ago. I am supporting Chuy because he is the right candidate for our neighborhood. He has promised to hire 1000 new Police Officers that our community desperately needs. He grew up in a real Chicago neighborhood, attended St. Rita High School, is way more in tune with our community than Rahm. Rahm is the wealthy Washington insider whose union credentials include making millions with his billionaire buddy Anti-Union Governor Bruce Rauner, passing American job killer NAFTA, saying F***

*the United Auto Workers and telling Chicago Teacher's Union
President Karen Lewis "F*** you Lewis". I admire all leaders
in Organized Labor Unions. Many unions are supporting Chuy
and the ones who are not have no reason to be anti Chuy. In his
30-year public service Chuy has a 100% pro union voting record. I
was proud to have Chuy march in the South Side Irish St. Patrick's
Day Parade. He got genuine rousing cheers all along the Parade
route. Chuy has also gotten that kind of reception each of the many
times he has visited the 19th Ward. The current mayor does not
get that kind of reception in our neighborhood and our alderman
did not even endorse him until after his own election was over.
The paper says that I am a lawyer and a boxing coach. It is true
that I earn my living as an attorney but as a boxing coach I do not
earn a penny. I use boxing to give back to the community. For over
20 years I have served as a volunteer boxing coach at the West
Englewood Boys Club, Leo High School and the Celtic Boxing Club.
Through amateur boxing shows I have helped raise hundreds of
thousands of dollars for worthy causes and charities including the
St. Baldrick's Foundation, the Mercy Home, the Irish American
Foundation, the National Italian American Sports Hall of Fame,
Leo High School, the West Englewood Boys Club, the Officer
John Hurley Family Fund, Catholic Charities, the Illinois State
Crime Commission/Police Athletic League of Illinois, the Tommy
Z Foundation, the Charlie Weiss Hannah and Friends Autism
Foundation and many others. I have also had the opportunity to
have inner city youth train alongside Chicago Police Officers and
Chicago Firefighters for the Battle of the Badges. The newspaper
may want to bash me for political reasons but I am blessed and
grateful for the support of friends in the community. My support
for Chuy is based solely on my wanting my 3-year-old grow up in
a neighborhood that I grew up in.*

I post this on my Facebook page where I post lots of campaign
stuff, i.e.; pro-Chuy, anti-Rahm quips.

Later in the day I get "private message" from Tim Novak of the

Sun-Times who wrote the front page smear story. I've never met this douchebag and we certainly are not "friends" on Facebook, but he seems to think he can approach me.

Tim Novak

Still waiting for Pickle Joyce to return the phone messages left at his law firm days before the story ran.

Mike Houlihan

Oh that old trick, Hey Mr. Big Shot investigative reporter, if you really wanted to talk to him you would have found a way to call him directly. Please save your bullshit for somebody who buys it.

*   *   *

When a reporter doesn't want to print a comment from somebody he is slandering, he will call the guy at a number he knows won't reach him and leave a message to cover his ass so he can say, "Mike Joyce couldn't be reached for comment."

Novak is a weasel, doing the bidding of his boss weasel Rahm Emanuel, who counts Sun-Times owners Michael Ferro and Michael Sacks as two of his biggest donors. Sacks is Rahm's largest single contributor, to the tune of $1, 056, 287 bucks, according to the Tribune. Sacks phones Rahm at least twice a day according to Chicago Magazine, who refer to him as "The Rahm Whisperer". The smear on Pickle and his family was probably triggered by one of those phone calls, cuz nothin' is on the square.

That's not journalism, it's gerbilism.

A gerbil. Photo courtesy of Gerbil Centerfolds.

Friday, April 3, 2015
Good Friday
Chicagoland

Nine shooting victims, two murders including Jerome Anderson, 21, shot in Washington Park, and Azun Buckner, 18, gunned down in Englewood.

I'm scheduled to staff Chuy for the final fish fry at the Irish American Heritage Center tonight.

Meet up with Cyril at Heritage Center and he tells me Clem called to cancel. I call Shaffer, then receive call from Andrew Sharp, then Cyril texts Chuy who responds and sends his regrets, feeling sick, doesn't want to screw up next three days. "Please tell Houli I'm sorry"

Class guy, but this is another example of fumbling on the goal line.

The Heritage Center is packed and Chuy could have picked up some votes here for sure. The crowd would like to see another Catholic on Good Friday for cripesakes!

Talk to Pickle on the way home, he's all steamed about Josh Kilroy, Chuy campaign slug, showing up at his office on 111th Street and telling his guys at the Celtic Boxing Office "I'm the boss". I'm sure those guys didn't take that well. Josh is lucky they didn't grab him right there and pants him and toss him out on to 111th Street. Who does he think he is? Oh yeah, Schaffer's brother in law!

Pickle is also upset with screw ups with the door hangers and the mailing, that the campaign now refuses to pay for. Pickle says, "It's over" once again and then becomes incoherent and I tell him "I'm driving into my garage now, I'll talk to you later." He's not being very positive, but then again I don't have all the information, and don't want it!

Holy Saturday April 4, 2015
Chicagoland

Six victims, including Milon L. Carvis 42, shot in the chest and killed in Auburn/Gresham, and Martell J. Lawrence, 16, shot in the head and murdered in Englewood.

I've pitched the campaign about having Chuy do another tour through the bars of Western Avenue tonight when the NCAA Finals are on the TV and the bars will be packed.

Helen from scheduling calls me this morning, "we want to do 19th Ward event during the NCAA playoffs as suggested". All set up for 8:30PM after Andrew Sharp sends me a note saying 'what time, we don't want to get there when everybody is hammered." I guess that's what he thinks of 19th warders.

We tell Alma, another scheduler, 8:30 is perfect, figure we'll hit Cork and Kerry, Keegan's Dingers, TR's, maybe Ken's even to shake hands and say hello.

Then they cancel . . . again, too sick . . . WTF!

Clem you asshole, ever heard of sucking it up?

"He's too sick."

I text Chuy, "Chuy, we got a bunch of guys up at Cork & Kerry, please don't be a pussy, be a Mustang and come by for ten-minute photo op, do a shot and go home!"

"You don't have to talk, just smile."

No response.

Sunday April 5, 2015
Easter Sunday

8 shooting victims today.

Easter Monday April 6, 2015
Election Eve

Two teenagers, 16 and 14, shot today in Englewood.

Started the day with texts to Chuy and assorted campaigners to try and get him to come out to 19th ward for final NCAA game and hit some of the bars, maybe get on TV. They seem to go for it, then Alma calls me and says he will be there in twenty minutes. WTF?

This is the kind of bullshit we've had to deal with throughout the campaign, no coordination, too many chiefs, not even Indians.

We finally get it figured out, and arrange to meet at Ken's around 7:30PM. I call Pickle trying to get a crowd there, he's not coming!

I haul ass up to Ken's and park and walk in and find a handful of regulars, fortunately all friends of mine, sitting at the bar. Well if this is it, this is it. I've got some Hall of Fame Southsiders at the bar, Skip Carey, retired copper and former saloon owner, Rick Leonard real estate artist and sometime bartender, Byron Bradley, retired copper and now lawyer, and of course our host Jackie Casto, the proprietor of Ken's.

Chuy shows up at Ken's with about ten people including his wife

Evelyn, and I don't know the rest of them. They all seem to know each other and we got the big game on the TVs but that's about it crowd-wise.

Well let's eat and drink, for tomorrow we . . . don't say it.

I sit at the head of the table and introduce Chuy to the gang.

Skip Carey, Rick Leonard, Chuy, and Byron Bradley at
Ken's-photo by Houli

In spite of the absence of a crowd, we're having a great time, final night of the campaign. I'm shooting the biscuit with a couple of young guys at the table who are probably young Commies and I tell them, "Just remember this, nothin' is on the square. There's an old story about the wizened old copy editor at the newspaper telling his young reporters, 'There's only two things on the up and up . . . Mother's Day and mountain climbing---and we ain't too sure about Mother's Day.'"

When I first returned home to Chicago from 12 years in New York City, I was here to produce and direct a play with music, THE

51ST WARD, by former NBC political commentator Peter Nolan. We raised about $150 grand to stage the show and my brother Danny invested in it and got many of his pals to invest as well. When he asked me how we could project if it was going to make any money, I told him, "Well that's up to the critics."

I'd been enslaved to the world of the theatre, brainwashed actually, for over a decade at that point and honestly believed that everything is legit, especially with show biz and theatre critics.

My brother asked, "Can't somebody grease the critics?" I scoffed, "No way, it doesn't work that way!"

Danny laughed, "It doesn't? What if the critic wants to hang on to his job, I'll bet if he got a phone call from his boss letting him know he better take care of a friend or he will be out pounding the sidewalk, that he would give it a good review. "

He was right of course, and he knew guys at the newspapers, guys who hired the theatre critics, that it was that simple, kind of an insurance policy. But I forbad it because "it's just not done."

Foolish youth, the show got some lukewarm reviews in spite of its brilliance, and closed in three or four weeks, and we were out $150,000 and learned a valuable lesson. Nothing is on the square, especially in Chicago.

Now Chuy is shooting the breeze with the boys at the bar after dinner, talking about his days at St. Rita. He seems relaxed, tired but ready for the whole thing to be over, one way or another. His wife is so lovely, Evelyn, she has MS, and through it all has been a rock, God love her. I think about that little shit Phil Ponce trashing them over their son and I would love to cut his tongue out and do an Irish dance on it.

Before they leave, Chuy and Evelyn graciously pose for a photo with Jackie Casto and our waitress Lauren. Jackie, if you are reading this, I better see this photo on your frickin' wall at Ken's!

I felt that I should do something symbolic to help inspire Chuy on this final night but wasn't sure how to go about it. Then I feel the rosary in my pocket, I'd bought it at St. Odilo's for a buck, it was green plastic, but I'd worked those beads myself for the last 82 days. I handed it to him, "Here take this with you, it's an Irish rosary."

He seemed touched, "Thank you Houli." I didn't tell him it wasn't from Ireland. Hey it was green and it was owned by me once, so that made it Irish!

Our waitress Lauren, Chuy, Evelyn Garcia and Jackie
Casto at Ken's-photo by Houli

Then everybody saddles up and a kid from the
campaign picks up the check. Last words I hear from Chuy before he leaves is, "Make sure you leave a big tip!"

Tuesday April 7, 2015
Chicagoland
Election Day

Louis Walker, 28, shot in the chest and murdered today in Uptown.

Went to eight o clock mass at St. Odilo's with my lovely wife Mary, drove her to my son, Paddy's house, took my daughter in law Haleigh to the El, went home, stopped at Goodwill and bought two pair of pants, then back to get granddaughter Charlotte for kindergarten at noon, then back home, took a nap, then picked up Charlotte from school, went to Burger King with her, back to her house, went for a walk with her, went home and got ready. Crawford called me three times, picked him up at James Joyce pub in Berwyn as he exited the train, so we could head downtown together.

Pickle called, says he's not going tonight, "don't want to be a distraction"

Election night for Chuy is at The UIC Forum, a huge joint, probably don't need that much space, but they do serve beer, that you have to BUY!

Tried to get a VIP pass for Cyril earlier in the day but was stonewalled by Schaffer, then got there, talked to Tara, "we don't have room for everybody", yeah that sounds familiar

We go to check-in table and while the girl is distracted, we grabbed 2 VIP passes off the table and walked away as me and Crawford draped them over our necks.

Met up with Cyril, he's already wearing his VIP pass that he talked the lady into giving him, got beers. Saw Patrick Fitzmaurice in the crowd, the very outspoken CFD EMS Field Chief, who hates Rahm, he did not look happy, "We're not doing good", showed me his cell phone. I couldn't read what he showed me, but I could tell it wasn't good news.

It's pretty early I'm thinkin', too call it, and then my sons text me, "wbbm is calling it for rahm". It's not even 8PM and my kids start texting me like I died or something. Bad moon risin'!

Cyril, Houli, and Crawford on election night.
Photo courtesy of Mike Houlihan

We walk into the great hall and there was a singing duo of 17-year-old girls onstage, what the hell is this?

Saw Jesse Jackson in the crowd sniffing out the cameras. It's hard to get any information, and these stupid musical acts keep coming onstage as if we're supposed to give two shits about them.

Then this douchebag hip hop artist rapper gets up there and he is just awful, and now the hubbub in the crowd is spreading rapidly, "Bad news, we're all getting news that it's over.", and Mr. Hip Hop says, "Hey I know you all is interested in your political stuff, but you gotta work with me here!"

I'll give you something to work with, you jagoff!

The whole thing was totally fecking awful. I had to get out of there, so I walked into the hallway in search of another beer, maybe I'm dreaming this.

But we walk into hall again and hear this woman onstage saying "Chuy has called Rahm to concede and he will be here in the building in about an hour, in the meantime here's some more music!"

I turn to Cyril and Crawford, "Let's get the fuck outta here!"

We leave and go to the Billy Goat on Madison, hardly anybody there. We get burgers and head over to the bar and order beers. It's a few laughs with Cyril. We're watching Chuy's concession speech on TV, no sound, but we can see Clem with a big shit-eating grin on his face behind Chuy.

Cyril asks through his Roscommon brogue, "What the fuck is he smiling' about?"

What the fuck indeed.

*   *   *

EPILOGUE

YOU KNEW HOW this story was going to end before we even started. I understand that. Hopefully we both have learned a few things while looking back.

We lost the runoff election by roughly 65,000 votes, about 11% of the votes cast made the difference. We did see a path to victory, but as the saying goes, "the best laid plans of mice and men oft go awry." Not sure there was even a plan to begin with.

Inept campaign management, the media complicit in unquestioning loyalty to a tyrant, and millions of dollars spent portraying Chuy as an incompetent immigrant all led to this.

Most important is that Rahm Emanuel is still the mayor of this once great city. That's something we will all have to live . . . or die with.

In May of 2015 Moody's Investors Service cut the rating of all of Chicago's municipal bonds to "junk".

In order to staunch the hemorrhaging expense of employee pensions, Emanuel approved a record breaking property tax increase of $543 million dollars. The Tribune headline said it all: "The tab on Emanuel's series of tax hikes: $1,700 a year for average family".

But even if you could afford that, odds are also pretty good that you're going to get shot in Chicago, maybe even murdered.

As I write this, over 700 people have been killed by violence this year, over 138 have been murdered on the same block they live on, and over "381 killed from injuries they suffered within two miles of their home address." Those stats come from the Sun-Times of November 21, 2016. Chicago finished up 2016 with 762 murders!

Murder in Chicago is up by 54% over last year.

That blood is on your hands Rahm Emanuel. You may escape jail with the help of your high powered friends, but your stay in hell will be eternity.

Because you didn't give a shit.

Late in 2015 karma started kicking in on Rahm.

Barbara Byrd Bennett, his hand-picked Chicago Public Schools CEO was indicted by the feds and pled guilty to wire fraud and trying to siphon off a 2.3 million kickback of a 23 million dollar no-bid contract she had steered to her pals. She was sentenced to 4.5 years in prison.

Then it came to light that this mayor covered up and suppressed the release of a police dashcam video of a cop murdering a black teenager, Laquan McDonald. Rahm orchestrated a $5 millions payoff to the mother of the kid as well, and kept that quiet too. Either one of those stunts would have lost him the election and Chuy would now be mayor.

To save his ass Rahm threw Cook County States Attorney Anita Alvarez under the bus, along with his hand-picked police superintendent Garry McCarthy, who famously said at a press conference before he was shit-canned, "The mayor has my back!" Ha, at that point most of us had already figured out he was going to get the axe, right in the back that the mayor supposedly had! What kind of cop could he have been not to see that coming?

Last December 2015, the New York Times called for Rahm to resign in the aftermath of the cover-up of the cop shooting video and hush money payment to the mother.

But still he reigns, dancing his way through the shit storm.

My friend Patrick Fitzmaurice opined to me the other day, "*Trust me, the day McCarthy knew about that video, Rahm knew about that video, within ten minutes, and he told him to dump it, you know he did.*

They obstructed justice. Why doesn't Trump bring in the Feds to investigate obstruction of justice? He lied.

Every day I have shootings, I'm having three and four and five shootings on a winter day. It's unheard of, our murder total in January is higher than it's ever been".

In February a two-year-old boy was murdered sitting in the back of his gang banger father's car. This summer it's going to get a lot worse.

The ascent of Rahm Emanuel since leaving the White House in 2010 to run for Mayor has been marked by chicanery, perfidy, and a preening over confidence. His time spent in the shadow of the Clintons and Obamas, was the grooming of a scoundrel. He learned to lie at their laps.

Like MacBeth, he is driven only by "vaulting ambition, which o'erleaps itself, and falls on the other" side, unhorsed with corpses all about him.

Through it all he has exhibited a profound paucity of character, very quick with the crocodile tears when all the dead black children are mentioned, but he's gone to the well too many times with that stunt.

When they build his statue it won't take much. I think back to the video of Rahm watching a summer concert, Robin Thicke singing "Blurred Lines" at Taste of Chicago. The Mayor in his shirt sleeves, knowing somebody's camera was on him, as he peeled off his tie, slipped it into his back pocket and grooved to the beat, and became the real Rahm, an effeminate tiny dancer humping a chair in Grant Park.

That's the image he leaves behind.

Will Rahm run for re-election?

Why not?

Are the people of Chicago that stupid? Or don't they care? Will they once again pull the lever for the nine-digit midget?

They might.

After all, this is Chicago, and nothin's on the square.

＊　＊　＊